LITERARY TRANSLATION AND FOREIGN RIGHTS

FIND TRANSLATORS, ENTER NEW MARKETS, AND MAKE MORE MONEY WITH LITERARY TRANSLATIONS

S C SCOTT

CREATIVE MINDS MEDIA

Literary Translation and Foreign Rights: How to Find Translators, Enter New Markets, and Make More Money with Literary Translations

Copyright © 2017 by S. C. Scott

All rights reserved. No part of this publication may be reproduced, stored in a retrieval system, or transmitted in any form or by any means—electronic, mechanical, recording, or otherwise—without the prior written consent of the copyright holder and publisher. The scanning, uploading and distribution of this book via the Internet or any other means without the permission of the publisher is illegal and punishable by law.

Please purchase only authorized electronic editions, and do not participate in or encourage electronic piracy of copyrighted materials. Your support of the author's rights is appreciated.

Published by Creative Minds Media

eBook ISBN: 978-1988272-44-3

Paperback ISBN: 978-1988272-43-6

How to Find Translators, Enter New Markets, and Make More Money with Literary Translations

Ready, Set, Translate!

The Indie Publishing Gold Rush is not over…

In fact, it's just beginning in non-English language markets. Find new readers, new markets, and make more money by translating your books into other languages. It's easier than you think!

Learn how to

- Identify hot global markets for your genre
- Source the best translators
- Translate your books with zero upfront investment
- Protect and exploit your rights
- Generate multiple streams of income with your books
- Gain new readers, reach new markets, and make more money!

Once you read this book you'll wish you had started sooner…but it's never too late! In fact, there's never been a better time to find new markets, gain new readers, and make more money!

1
THE LITERARY TRANSLATION LANDSCAPE

Welcome to the wonderful world of literary translation. Today it is easier than ever before to share your books with readers all over the world.

I wrote this book for authors like you who want to enter new markets and grow sales and readership. When I explored translations and foreign rights alternatives several years ago, I couldn't find much information anywhere. I found my answers by trial and error, and what little information I gleaned was usually outdated. It certainly wasn't geared towards indie authors in the 21st century.

I kept this book as short as possible so that you can use it as a guide for each topic as you progress through your own translation adventure. I have assumed that you have already independently published your own books and are therefore well-versed in the subject. If this isn't the case, there are many excellent books covering publishing and related topics, so I haven't reproduced that information here.

I highly recommend reading this book in its entirety before starting your translation project. Having the big picture before you start will save you time and effort later. This book starts at a high level overview before getting into specifics because I think that is the best way to grasp the concepts behind successful translations. I hope that it also instills you with confidence. Most of all I want to save you from some of my early mistakes. Once we look at the fundamentals we will do a deep dive into the details.

There is no need to take notes. Any questions you have early on will be answered in the later chapters which provide all the detail you need to get started. There are also checklists at the end of the book summarizing all the key points.

If you do decide to read the book in a different order, that's fine too. Everyone learns and absorbs information differently.

Thank you for reading this book. I hope you find it useful.

Multiple Streams of Income

As authors, we tend to think of our books as extensions of ourselves. They are in the sense that we have created intellectual property. But they are also products that can take on many physical forms. Once you adopt this mindset, you might ask yourself why you never considered translation before.

Think of each book as an individual asset from which additional derivative rights can be created. Most authors dream of getting their books made into movies or TV series, and many already do paperbacks and audiobooks. The one area that is commonly overlooked is translation. Translate into 9 additional languages and your one book suddenly becomes 10 books. It's like multiple streams of income on steroids!

But wait—it gets better!

Each translated book can also be turned into other products. You can create 9 new audiobooks in each language too. Suddenly your novel isn't just an English language eBook, paperback, and audio book anymore. When you translate into 9 additional languages you have (9+1) x 3 formats = 30 products instead of just 3. Pretty amazing, isn't it?

Maybe you had already reached this conclusion but figured chances of success were slim for all but the most successful bestselling authors. While your book should have at least some commercial success as the basis to assume decent sales in other markets, there are plenty of books with great potential for foreign translations that weren't number one bestsellers in their original language. Your book could be one of them!

All you have to do is find translators, sign contracts with them, and wait for your translated book. It's almost that easy...but not quite. You must do a bit of legwork to ensure you end up with a quality product. Your author name is your brand, and your success or failure depends on a great translation.

A great translation means finding a talented translator, but choosing a bad translator can ruin your reputation. Searching and screening translators can be time-consuming at first but is well worth the effort. A good translator can open up new markets for you and bring your books to a whole new world of readers to read and enjoy. Some might even become your biggest fans.

If you are reading this book, I assume that you are either:

- An independent author looking to expand into other markets
- A traditional author who has retained her foreign rights and wants to learn how to monetize them
- Either a new or established author who is seeking to understand all her options and potential new markets and ways to reach them

Maybe your book is a bestseller in your native language, or you are still growing your readership. Regardless of your current status, it is always a good idea to explore how you can take charge of your career. That includes expanding by translating into other languages.

Trouble is, you don't know where to start. Or should you even start? Sometimes translation can be financially worthwhile, other times not, so it's important to understand your own particular earning potential as well as the potential investment of time, money, and effort you will need to put in. Knowing your options dramatically increases your chances of success.

This goal of this book is to give you an overview of the market and the knowledge and tools needed to assess your chances of success in a foreign market. Even if your foreign rights have already been contracted to a publisher, it's important to know what your options are. There are many choices for your existing books and future books in the rapidly changing publishing world of today.

Knowing what options are available to you can help guide your decisions going forward. If you have already assigned your foreign language rights, you likely never gave them much thought. In the past, these foreign rights would have been considered "found money" since these were markets inaccessible to you as an individual author. Or maybe you are an indie author debating whether to sell your foreign rights or keep them yourself.

Whatever the case, language, cultural, and physical barriers used to mean that you couldn't enter foreign markets on your own. You needed an agent and an interested foreign publisher to publish your book in a foreign language, and even then, it was rarely viable financially. All that has changed.

Technology has made indie global publishing both physically possible and economically viable. There are many ways to translate your book into multiple languages and the method you choose can make all the difference as to whether your book generates profits or not. It's vitally important to understand the options available for your already published books, as well as for books published in future.

You might even want to get these rights reverted back to you. In any event, the material in this book will give you greater insight into how you can monetize your foreign rights going forward. Knowing all the options helps you to make an informed decision. There is no one right answer, only the arrangement that works best for you.

Times Are Changing

Not too long ago, the only way to get your books translated into foreign languages was through an agent or publishing company. You assigned your foreign translation rights to your publisher, who then sold the rights to an agent or publishing company in another country. There were so many people involved, each taking a cut so that it rarely resulted in anything but a minuscule financial return for the author.

Authors sometimes assume that there is no money in translations, but often it is simply that the money is being divided up too many ways, with only a small percentage actually left for the author at the bottom of the food chain. Authors with foreign rights deals often see the net proceeds without any detailed accounting, and might even remain unaware of the gross earnings of their books.

The process is further complicated by language barriers, bureaucracy, and red tape. Many authors with foreign translations of their work often never received anything beyond a small initial advance. Add in sparse or nonexistent sales reporting, and it's no wonder that many authors believe that foreign translations aren't worth the time or effort.

Technology has changed all that. The Internet has connected translators and authors like never before. We also have automated reporting, online sales platforms, and efficient distribution systems. No longer do we need someone in the middle to arrange the deal and take their cut. You can deal directly with a translator and publish your book exactly the same way as you do for your English versions because technological advances have removed most of the barriers.

The point is that things are changing quickly and more opportunities open up for authors every day. It's more important than ever to make sure your decisions are informed ones, regardless of what path you choose. I, for one, want to be at the top of the food chain as the creator of the work. Don't you?

I hope this book helps you to avoid some of my newbie mistakes and more importantly, to capitalize on the enormous value of your intellectual property. You have the potential to make much more money with your books by translating them into other languages.

Why I Translate

I write mysteries and thrillers under a pen name. I publish independently on many sales platforms, including major ones like Amazon, Apple iBooks, Barnes & Noble, Google Play, and Kobo, as well as with some smaller retailers.

I began translating my books several years ago. At that time, there was little to no information available online, so I learned by trial and error. There are huge opportunities for forward-looking authors with an open mindset, but it does involve a little work. By sharing my experiences with you, I hope to make it as easy and seamless as possible, and maybe even establish a fast track to success.

I believe in having multiple streams of income, or keeping my eggs in many baskets, so to speak. While I am a full-time writer, writing is not my only source of income. In addition to my writing income, I also operate a small business part-time and earn passive income from my investments.

As an investor, I know to diversify my investments to spread the risk of any one investment going terribly bad and losing everything. But diversification isn't just to be safe—it can also expose you to more opportunities. I have followed the same strategy with my books: make strategic investments, be open to new opportunities, and reduce risk wherever I can.

I believe in diversification, not just to spread risk, but also to maximize opportunity.

Aside from writing in multiple series and genres, there are other ways to diversify such as audiobooks, paperbacks, and hardbacks. Publishing on many sales platforms instead of being exclusive to one platform is another way to diversify. Of course, there are arguments the other way, and some authors find they maximize their revenue by concentration on one platform exclusively.

You can even do both. Maybe you decide to be Kindle Select

exclusive for your English language books but sell widely for your foreign translations. There are so many ways to expand your writing business, and translation is one of the best ways to expand into new markets and further monetize your literary assets.

Every new literary asset you have potentially expands your audience. Increasing your product line also increases your income, at least in theory. Your work has to be marketable, of course. But marketability in one language does not guarantee it will be popular in other languages, countries, or regions. Both fiction and nonfiction tastes vary widely by country, region, and language, something you need to consider before you decide to take the plunge. But the market is there if you have a good book in the right genre and language.

Romance is one genre that seems to be popular everywhere, but that broad category has many smaller subgenres and niches that vary wildly in popularity amongst different cultures, languages, and readers. If you write science fiction or fantasy, or mysteries and thrillers, there are plenty of markets for you too.

Maintain Control

Technology enables authors to take control of their intellectual property and reach more people today than at any point in history. Today many authors publish directly to retail platforms like Amazon, Apple, and others, bypassing the traditional publishing route. A few short years ago, traditional publishers were the gatekeepers, deciding who got published and when.

Some of the chosen few would also have their books translated into other languages in "rights deals", where the publisher would assign these rights in exchange for a cut. In the end, though, most of those authors saw very little of that money.

All that has changed. Every great opportunity also brings new issues and pitfalls to consider. Some people like the control of being hands-on, while others would prefer to have someone else navigate for them. The good news is that you can follow whatever path suits you best. This book gives you the information you need to make an informed decision.

I have translated my books into many languages over the last few years with plans to translate many more. I am fortunate that my native language is English, the first language where eBooks have enjoyed wide adoption. I am convinced that the current independent publishing environment is just the beginning. There are many more markets and readers looking for books written by authors like me. It's great to be able to decide what books I want to sell and in which markets. I like the ability to make my own decisions and adapt quickly if market conditions change.

More Products to Sell

You've already written your book and have a product to sell. Why not translate your book into as many languages as you can? Each language represents a new stream of income. All you need is someone to translate it into another language. Simple, right?

You would think so, but…

Translation, like writing, is an art. If you've ever used a machine translation tool like Google Translate and have an understanding of both the source and destination languages, you'll know that each language has nuances that are easily—and often—lost in translation.

Sentence structure, verb conjugation, and meanings can differ across languages. Even within the same language, meanings and dialects can vary. American and British English for example, or Spanish in Spain versus South America. Minor differences are usually understood across regions, but major differences might not be tolerated or even understood. Even if they are understood, you don't want to jolt a reader out of a story with unfamiliar terms or sentence structure. You want your book to flow the same way it does in the language you wrote it in.

Your translator is effectively rewriting your book from beginning to end, so it is important to ensure you find someone who translates not only the meaning of the words but also the tone and mood of the story. A translated mystery/thriller must keep the same suspense and tension for a nail-biting read.

A good translation sells many more books than a mediocre one. A bad translation will tarnish your reputation and turn readers off from buying your future books. Fortunately, there are ways to ensure you get the former, which we will explore in later chapters. A lucky few of you will find a translator so talented that the translated version might turn out even better than the original text!

I'll give you all the information you need to find top-notch translators and take your books global. Now let's get started!

2

WHY TRANSLATE? AND WHY YOU SHOULD

There are many reasons to translate your books into other languages. You will find new readers. People who do not speak or read in your language will never discover your work unless it is written in a language they can understand. Translation allows you to step over language barriers and connect with readers that you would otherwise never reach.

The most commonly-held belief is that books must already be bestsellers to make translation worthwhile, and that even then they are a bit of a gamble. I think that's an overstatement, but your books should be at least popular within your genre before you consider moving into new (and often smaller) markets. A smaller market in and of itself does not mean that sales will be lower for your book, however. Often there is less competition and you can charge higher prices, something that most people overlook when they estimate the value of their foreign rights. But you still need to take a critical look at your books when considering the markets you wish to enter. This is an important first step to take before moving forward.

Books that are not big sellers in their original source language can turn into blockbuster hits in another language. This is the exception rather than the norm, but it happens more often than you might think. I certainly don't recommend translating a poorly selling book. Often it will sell poorly in other languages for the same reasons as in the original language. But if you have a well-written book with good customer reviews and decent sales, there is potential for that book to sell well in another market. There are many examples of books that have done exactly this.

There are other considerations besides current sales. Markets very dramatically by language, country, and genre. For example, cozy mysteries are very popular in English but do not sell well in Spanish. Romance is the most popular genre in just about every language and country, but success in the many romance subgenres varies widely for reasons of taste and cultural mores.

Thrillers and crime novels seem to be most popular in the northern hemisphere. Maybe it's those long winters? Finally, just like fashion, trends come and go. The best way to see if translation is worthwhile for you is to study the market and stores in your target language. If there are books similar to yours, then chances are it is worth a look.

As of this writing, Amazon is the dominant store in most English-speaking countries, though Kobo is number one in Canada and popular in Australia and New Zealand. In North America and the UK, we tend to see the world through Amazon-colored glasses, but Amazon is not number one in many countries. In most countries, Amazon does not even have a store. In France for example, Fnac.com is the most popular online bookstore, though Amazon is close behind. Italy has many bookstores including Mondadori, but Amazon is very popular.

Translated books can have prices that are much higher in some languages compared to others. It's mostly a matter of supply and demand. English, the most mature eBook market with the greatest supply and selection, also has the lowest prices and highest competition. Many authors focus only on the largest markets, such as the English and German languages, but in some instances they could find easier profits in other underserved markets where their books will stand out against the crowd. A popular book in the right genre can command a premium price, often 9.99 or higher for a well-written novel. I'd rather have 70% of $9.99 than 30% of 99 cents. I have to sell more than 23 books at 99 cents versus one at $9.99 to earn the same amount of money.

Another added bonus to foreign translations is added visibility if your destination language is a less competitive market. It's easier to hit a bestseller list in a less crowded market. Could your book be a contender?

Check the bestsellers in the language you are considering to see if books similar to yours are popular. Book bestseller status can also vary dramatically from store to store within each country, so be sure to find out which stores are the most popular in each particular country and use those as your guide. Then look at which genres are selling well there. Is your genre one of them? If it is, translation could be a worthwhile venture.

It's also important to remember that a #1 bestseller on Amazon Brazil is nothing like a #1 Amazon USA bestseller in terms of sales volume. The market in Brazil is much smaller in terms of readers and the selling price is much lower. That means less money for you.

On the other hand, there are also fewer Portuguese language books in the store when compared to English books on the American Amazon.com site. This lower sales volume means that it takes fewer sales to hit the #1 bestseller status. That means greater in-store visibility for you, and visibility in and of itself will lead to more book sales.

All of this is meant to illustrate that there are several variables at work. What seems like a too-small market can actually be profitable when all these factors are considered, especially in a growing market. But in the meantime don't assume that a Brazilian bestseller will allow you to make hundreds of thousands of dollars. It won't. At least not yet.

You probably know that *The Girl with the Dragon Tattoo* and Stieg Larsson's other books were originally published in Swedish. They sold well in Sweden, but the German translation didn't really get noticed. Then they were translated into English and sales skyrocketed in North America, the UK and...the German translation in Germany. The catalyst was the English version, which prompted German readers to finally notice the books in German. Getting your books into many markets can have exponential effects. Maybe your book will be the next big success.

Past, Present, and Future

The only way to get into foreign markets a few years ago was through a foreign rights agent, usually through your regular agent. Then you paid a percentage of your foreign publisher advance to your agent and the foreign agent. The idea of paying large commissions was acceptable because there was no other alternative. There were many people in the middle and each one took a cut. The end result was that most authors never saw a penny beyond a small advance.

Many authors think foreign translations are not profitable because they haven't been profitable for *them*. But they are profitable —for the people in between—your publisher, the foreign publisher, and the one or two agents involved. If they weren't, your publisher wouldn't be so insistent on locking up your foreign rights when you sign a publishing contract.

Somebody is making money, and it's time for that someone to be you! Times are changing, and the model is changing too.

Way back in time when there was no Internet, none of this was possible. Even as recently as several years ago, it was difficult to get around language barriers. There was no such thing as self-publishing either. All that has changed, and self-publishers today have a world of opportunities never available before. Technology has broken down barriers and built platforms to enable us to reach more readers than ever.

Things as simple as Google Translate allow us to quickly and easily translate foreign languages into our own. The translation is usually quite literal so it's not exactly pretty, but it gets the job done. Suddenly with a mouse click on "translate" we can have a translation adequate enough to grasp the meaning of a website, article, or text very quickly. And just in case you're wondering, I want to make it clear that you should NEVER use Google Translate to translate your books! It can't possibly replace a literary translator. At least not yet.

Traditional Publishing and Foreign Rights Clauses

If you are traditionally published, your publishing contract typically assigns your rights to the publisher for 70 years plus life. Your whole life and maybe your children's too! That has always seemed draconian to me, but it's just the way things were. And still are. Because if you sell your foreign rights through your publisher, it's likely you'll have similar terms.

While the terms aren't the greatest, at least it's effortless for you. But is the net result worth the opportunity cost you have just signed away? How can you know what might have been? The royalty accounting is so opaque that you just might never know how much money you gave up—until you consider and compare it to the new options that are available to you today.

Advance aside, if you sell enough books to earn out your advance, you get a percentage of the publisher's net receipts from the retailer. It's usually a small percentage. Remember all those people in the middle? They always deduct their commissions and expenses out before the money reaches you, the creator of the book. That means a lot less money for you, the author.

One reason why many authors believe that foreign translations are not profitable is because they never see any money from it. They assume it is due to smaller markets or poor crossover of their work into other languages. Some of this is true, of course. But often the primary reason is that the residual amount left over for the author is meager once all the middleman fees are paid.

There are definite advantages to the traditional arrangement. You sign and forget, and leave the publishing and promotional worries to someone else. You might have greater print sales opportunities with a traditional publisher because they can get your books into more stores (in theory, at least). But today, self-published authors can get their books into the same distribution channels and catalogs as traditionally published authors. This could still vary a little by country, but the barriers are quickly collapsing. I'm guessing that any advantage traditional publishing holds over independent publishing will disappear within the next 3 to 5 years at most.

Naturally, most authors would rather write than deal with all the complexities of publishing and marketing. If you're fortunate, you get a check every once in a while. And while you won't be consciously aware that you are leaving money on the table, there is another disadvantage to selling your rights: losing control and visibility over your sales. We will get into this in detail later in the book.

If you're traditionally published, you likely already signed over foreign translation rights for some or all of your books. Most authors do when they sign their publishing contract. Remember the multiplying factor I mentioned earlier of 3 books and 9 new languages? You really are surrendering a lot of potential future income when you give up these rights. While it is an amazing ego boost to sign with a publisher, it is even more thrilling to see money accumulating in your bank account. Knowing your options can help you to seize future opportunities.

It's a good idea to check your existing contracts to see what, if any, foreign rights you have signed and which rights are still within your own control. Then you will know which books you might be able to get translated yourself.

Legal terminology can be confusing at the best of times. It also varies by country, so it's always a good idea to review any contract with a lawyer before you sign. While your publisher and agent may be great people, they have their own vested interests in the contract aside from your interests. And while agents may be well-versed in publishing, they are not legal experts. A lawyer's opinion may seem expensive up front, but it will likely save or make you more money in the long run.

Full disclaimer: I am not a lawyer and this is not legal advice. I just believe that keeping control of your intellectual property always makes good business sense. As the saying goes, the devil is in the details.

If you have already signed a contract, you need to determine whether you have sold or assigned your rights. This distinction is very important. If you sold your rights, your contract could have terms specifying the right to copy, distribute, perform, etc. It is highly likely that you gave these rights to the publisher to exploit. If that is the case then you might have surrendered the right to make translations of your book.

Today it is more common to licence your rights. In this case you have granted a right to the publisher. It may limited in scope and time. However the terms can still be broad. Did you grant English ebook rights, or worldwide exclusive rights? It is important to consider how narrow or broad these licensing rights are in your particular contract. This is where legal advice before signing contracts can really pay off in the long term.

Also consider whether the publisher has both the expertise and intention to exploit the rights on your behalf. If not, you might be better off keeping them.

For future contracts, it is important to understand what you are getting and what you are giving up. Ask your agent about the pros and cons, but keep in mind that the agent has a vested interest in you signing with the publisher, since that is how they are compensated and earn a living. You might or might not have a lot of negotiating power, but it's always good to be well-informed. And since the publisher wants your book, you likely have more influence over the contract terms than you first think.

It is good practice to negotiate to give the publisher only the rights they are likely to pursue, rather than exclusive rights. If they don't provide specific details on what they will do with translation and other rights, assign them limited rights instead. Reserve rights for everything else, such as translation.

With so many opportunities today and in the near future, you or someone you hire can almost certainly monetize the rights more effectively. Times are changing, and you won't be the first author to ask for changes to your book's foreign rights contract.

One change you might want to consider is limiting the contract term. That way if you aren't happy with the results, you can contract with another publisher once the term is up, or manage the translation process yourself by following the steps in this book. A shorter contract term provides additional incentive for the publisher to promote the book early on.

Whether you choose to assign them to the publisher or keep them to monetize yourself, make it a conscious decision. Just because you aren't famous today doesn't mean you never will be. J.K. Rowling signed with a publisher for print rights but had the foresight to keep her eBook and other subsidiary rights. That one decision made her tens, if not hundreds, of millions of dollars.

Carrie Fisher of Star Wars fame signed away all her derivative rights for a small (by Hollywood standards) flat fee and was paid nothing further for all of the merchandise created in her image. She missed out on millions of dollars. Hers is an extreme example, but it's always difficult to predict what could become a blockbuster bestseller years into the future. Something similar could happen to you, and you can't erase the ink on that contract once you sign it.

Having said all that, if you're reading this book, chances are that you have already been thinking of taking more control of your foreign translation rights. There are ways to get your book into the hands of readers in foreign lands while maintaining control over your intellectual property.

This book was written primarily for the indie author, so it has a do-it-yourself focus, but we will look at all options so you can make informed decisions.

A World of Opportunity and Multiple Streams of Income

In addition to being an author, I think of myself as any other business owner looking for ways to expand and earn more money. Our books are intellectual property that can be turned into numerous new products and multiple income streams. I've always believed in diversification, and new markets via translation fits that model perfectly.

I also believe in that old adage: "Luck is what happens when preparation meets opportunity." Today is the perfect time to create your own luck by learning about the amazing opportunities that are available to authors like you today. Technology has given us the tools to profit from our intellectual property in ways that were impossible until now.

EBooks are becoming more and more popular in other languages and markets. Some areas of opportunity are obvious. Germany, for instance, has high eBook adoption, avid readers, and a relatively high number of readers with disposable income to spend money on books. Other attractive languages and markets are not so obvious.

Throughout this book, I use eBooks and books interchangeably, though eBooks currently represent the lion's share of books sold for an independently published author. EBooks also have fewer market, distribution, and technological barriers to get books into foreign markets. They are a low-cost, low-risk way for a reader to try new authors.

More people are reading eBooks every day on their e-readers, phones, and tablets. This is especially true in developing countries where supply and distribution constraints make paper books too expensive for most people. EBook markets can quickly become the dominant book form in these markets and provide great opportunities for authors. However, I always publish both eBook and print copies of all of my translations and recommend that you do the same. Print opportunities and barriers to distribution are coming down all the time, and with the Internet, paperbacks are only a click away from readers too.

It is important to study each language and market to gain an understanding of potential returns. However, it is not just the number of speakers of a particular language or market demographics that needs to be studied. A major consideration is consumer tastes. The popularity of reading as an entertainment choice varies widely by country, language, and demographic, so it is important to know your market before you delve into the time and expense of translation. There are huge opportunities but also pitfalls if you don't choose correctly.

The good news is that it is very easy to evaluate potential growth areas once you know where and how to look. This book has everything you need to make that happen. There has never been a better time to be an author, and there has never been a better time to translate your works into other languages.

3

GLOBAL TRANSLATION MARKETS – AN OVERVIEW

Translation opportunities vary dramatically by language, country, and genre. Market maturity also plays a major role. For instance, e-book adoption in the English-speaking markets of the United States and the United Kingdom is much more mature than in other languages and countries where digital books are just getting started.

The popularity of reading as an entertainment form varies widely too. Reading is not as popular in Arabic countries, for example, especially those with lower literacy rates. Indian readers overwhelmingly prefer nonfiction books over fiction. There are also many countries with either more conservative or more liberal tastes that will dictate whether a genre is more successful or less so.

This means that you should carefully study the markets by language and country and target your translation goals accordingly. Let's look at Germany, which is considered the second biggest market in terms of language after the U.S.

What types of books sell the best in Germany? A look at the top 100 books on Amazon.de shows that romance dominates the top 100 books, followed by thrillers. This is a snapshot at a point in time and things are always changing, but it gives you a good idea of whether your books are in the genres that have the greatest appeal to German readers.

If you write something more specialized like American Civil War history, your expectations should also be much higher in a market like the U.S. where this topic is understandably more popular, rather than outside it.

Once you determine that your genre fits the foreign market, consider your book's potential for success against other similar books. If your book does not sell well in the original language version, please think long and hard about assuming your results will be any better in a second language. In fact, they could be even worse if the market is smaller.

On the other hand, they could actually perform better than your English books. For instance, if you write crime fiction and find an underserved market in Danish, your translated books could find a competitive advantage by standing out in a niche market.

It's important to make informed choices to make the best use of time and money, both yours and your translator's. While the translator will be doing most of the work, they will rightfully expect their time investment to be worthwhile, especially if they are working on a royalty-share basis. And you, as the author will be spending time sourcing a good translator, formatting and publishing the book, getting new covers and promoting the translated book. You want to maximize your chances of success, and the first consideration is potential markets where your book will sell.

How to Evaluate Potential Markets

The method I use is to start with the largest markets and look at which genres sell the best. If my genre is one of them, then I dig down into the details including sub-genre at the biggest sales platforms in that country. Note that the most popular store is often not Amazon in countries outside the U.S. and the U.K. and bestseller genres can also vary greatly by sales platform.

I consider markets by country, not by language. For instance, the

U.S. and U.K. share the same language but have somewhat different tastes in genres. Spain and Mexico might share genre tastes (or not), but there are very distinct regional differences in terms of translation as well as pricing. The same book in a particular language might be profitable in one country but not in another.

This granular analysis isn't as time-consuming as it seems, and a bit of time spent studying each market will pay dividends for you later in terms of knowing where and what translations to prioritize.

At present, some of the largest book markets are the U.S., China, Germany, Japan, United Kingdom, and France. There are also other countries where eBooks are rapidly gaining traction, such as Italy. Smaller markets can be very attractive due to higher prices and lower competition. For example, Dutch readers are accustomed to paying somewhat higher eBook prices than in the U.S. because it is a much smaller market with fewer choices.

Some markets, like China, are huge, but prices are much lower, usually about 20% of U.S. prices. There are also significant barriers and limited points of market entry for an indie author. However in China, what you lose in price can potentially be more than made up with volume with the right book.

You will want to choose markets with good distribution channels readily available to sell your books. There is no point translating a book for a large market if you have no way to reach readers. While I would love to translate all my books into every possible language, this is neither practical nor financially viable.

Every market has its own unique opportunities—and pitfalls. Mature markets with greater e-book adoption usually mean lower prices, higher competition, and lower future growth potential. Early entry into a less mature market might mean less competition and less price sensitivity, but growth can be slow or might not happen as predicted. There is always the danger that a small market won't grow at all.

On the other hand, lower competition gives you more visibility, making it easier to build readership. Smaller markets can usually support higher prices, something authors often overlook when evaluating their foreign rights. On the flip side, some large markets have lower numbers of readers due to culture, cost, or competing entertainment choices. I won't go into detail here since things are constantly changing. Instead, I will share my method for choosing and prioritizing which languages to translate into.

Choosing Markets to Enter

Most authors will look at large markets and prioritize those for translation without considering smaller, niche markets that might actually result in greater profits. For example, most English-speaking authors look at Germany as the next most lucrative market for their books.

I evaluate a little differently, with a greater emphasis on markets with higher prices and lower competition, because I feel this gives me higher odds of success and better long-term earnings potential. Your results could vary, but the point is to consider many variables instead of just the market size and to be fully informed so you can make logical, well-reasoned choices based on the information available to you at the time.

The U.S. market, despite low-selling prices, a growth rate that has plateaued, and high competition, is still one of the best markets to be in, and might still represent the best choice from a profit perspective. But will it last?

Many top authors are finding that their books stay atop the charts for shorter periods and must be priced lower to achieve the same sales volumes they did a year ago. The English-language market overall is maturing and is glutted with books as it becomes easier than ever to publish. There are many other lucrative markets worth exploring.

What about huge untapped markets like China? There are many underserved markets that could become even more profitable in the coming years. The most successful authors will be the ones who enter the market early. But with unknowns comes risk, so I developed criteria to help me assess the risks and rewards of each global market.

I study markets first by language and then by dominant country.

Once I have identified markets where books in my genre are popular overall, I consider other factors.

Market Evaluation Criteria

My ideal market has the following features:

High prices – books command high selling prices

High growth – reading is widespread and steady or growing in popularity

Low competition – a low number of books to meet demand

Large Market – a large potential market of readers

Genre – I confirm that my chosen genre and sub-genre are among the most popular ones in that particular language and market and on that country's largest sales platforms.

A book that meets three or more of these criteria has good potential. It's hard to find markets with all of these features. If you do, then that is a market well worth exploring. It is also worth noting that a large market without any of the other factors can still be a good thing, but you will likely have to compete on price (have low-selling prices), and you will likely incur higher advertising costs to gain visibility as the market will be very competitive.

Here are a few examples of what I have found:

Chinese

High Growth

Low Competition

Large Market

Popular genres: romance, mysteries

Popular online stores: Baidu, Douban, Amazon.cn, Overdrive

Chinese represents a huge market with a very high growth rate. It is potentially much larger than the English market, but there are restrictions and censorship against certain types of books, especially those with political themes that could be considered critical of the Chinese state. The Chinese market is more conservative than that of the U.S. when it comes to romance. Many romance books will be considered too racy for the Chinese censors. Books about sensitive political or historical subjects wouldn't be acceptable either.

Prices are much lower than in the U.S., usually around $1/5^{th}$ of U.S. prices, offset by much higher volume.

There are both simplified (China) and traditional (Hong Kong and Taiwan) Chinese translations, so you will want to do both. It is difficult to impossible to distribute and sell Chinese translations in China because you need Chinese government issued ISBN's which are only issued to recognized Chinese publishing companies.

If you are outside of China, you need to find a translation solution that also provides both translation and distribution if you want to reach the majority of Chinese readers—those in Mainland China. I expect these choices to grow in the coming year and discuss existing options in the sales platforms section later in the book. Kobo has very recently added Taiwan distribution, so new channels are also opening up in that smaller market.

Dutch

High Prices
  High Growth
  Low Competition
  Popular genres: romance, thrillers
  Popular online stores: Bol.com, Kobobooks.com

Amazon has a Dutch store but it is not nearly as popular as Bol.com. The market here is small but the percentage of the population who read is quite high, and because native Dutch speakers number only about 25 million people, not as many books are translated into Dutch as other languages. Readers are also accustomed to paying higher prices.

Kobo has also just launched Kobo Plus, an eBook subscription service for 10 euros a month in both the Netherlands and Belgium. Belgium has two major languages: Dutch (a Flemish dialect) and French. Kobo Plus is a pilot rollout of Kobo's global subscription service, and I expect it will provide further demand for translated eBooks.

Belgian (Flemish) Dutch tends to be a bit more formal than Netherlands Dutch. Since the majority of Dutch speakers are in the Netherlands, I opted for a translator from the Netherlands.

French

High Prices
    Low Competition
    Popular genres: thrillers, romance
    Popular online stores: fnac.fr, amazon.fr, kobobooks.com

The French love their bookstores, but after a somewhat slow start, eBooks are finally starting to gain traction. This is a reasonably large but slow-growing market, one where eBooks are starting to gain favor with commuters. This is a market where you can still get in early to establish your name. I think it has very good long-term potential.

About 40% of native French speakers worldwide are in Europe, with Canada a distant second. French is also a very common second language in many parts of the world including former French colonies, particularly Africa.

I prefer translators from France simply because I find that their translations are more universally accepted. Bestselling books are often translated into both European French and Canadian French because both are sizeable markets, but the dialects are quite different. The Canadian dialect is not one that European French speakers want to read and vice-versa, but since the majority of native speakers are European, the European dialect tends to be more widely accepted elsewhere. Obviously there are even more French variations around the world, but these are the two largest groups.

German

High Growth
    Large Market

Popular genres: romance, science-fiction/fantasy, crime fiction

Popular online stores: Amazon.de, Tolino alliance (Thalia, Weltbild, Hugendubel, Buch.de, club.de, ebook.de, etc.)

The majority of German speakers reside in Germany, though there are also German speakers in Austria, Switzerland, and elsewhere. Though there are fewer regional variations in German versus other languages, I have opted for translators from Germany. One word of caution: if you contract with Germany-based contractors directly, be aware that under German law, the translator, not the author, owns the copyright of the translated book. This can have a significant impact, since the copyright holder will therefore hold the audiobook and other derivative rights of the translated book, not you.

One way around this is to make the contract "a work for hire", where the contractor (the translator) agrees to assign his rights to you, the author. As with any legal contracts, it is best to get legal advice if you are dealing directly with a German translator. German law might even supersede your contract terms, depending on the contract jurisdiction. Since laws vary and can change at any time, I avoid potential risks under this arrangement by using a third-party platform like as Babelcube, which employs a work for hire contract with the translator and has a contract dispute mechanism. More about Babelcube later.

Italian

High Growth
    High Prices
    Low Competition
    Popular genres: romance and more romance!
    Popular online stores: Amazon.it, Mondadori.it

Italian is a small but growing market with high eBook adoption and reasonably high prices. Although the market is somewhat small, reading is very popular in Italy. There are lots of bookstores, distribution channels, and book bloggers.

There are also many talented translators, so you can easily find a top-notch Italian translator at a reasonable rate. It is one of my favorite markets at the moment because there is not a lot of competition.

If I were to pick a market to start in today, it would be Italy.

Portuguese

Large Market

Popular genres: romance, nonfiction

Popular online stores: Livararia Cultura, Amazon.com.br, Apple iBooks, Google Play

The majority of native Brazilian speakers are from Brazil, with Portugal second at just a fraction of Brazil. The eBook market is growing in Brazil, but with a high proportion of free downloads and low prices. However, with such a large market and plenty of good translators available, it is a market you should not ignore. I expect it to evolve similar to the U.S. market as low-priced and highly competitive.

Brazil has a well-developed publishing sector. With the Brazilian economy in a downturn at present, there are lots of good Brazilian Portuguese translators available for freelance work.

I prefer a Brazilian-Portuguese native speaker for market size reasons.

Spanish

Large Market

Popular genres: Romance, historical fiction, fantasy

Popular online stores: Librerias Ghandi (Mexico) BajaLibros (South America), Amazon.es, Amazon.mx, Amazon.com

While Spanish is the second-most popular language globally behind Chinese in terms of native speakers, it does not convert into an equally large number of readers. For some reason, reading is not one of the most popular leisure activities in many Spanish-speaking countries. In addition, piracy is quite high in many South American countries, keeping sales low. With the exception of Spain, incomes in the Spanish-speaking countries also tend to be lower than in Europe and North America on average.

Most European Spanish readers are less accepting of non-European Spanish, such as Mexican or Latin American dialects. While there no significant language variations amongst countries, there are noticeable differences when it comes to grammar, word choice, formality, and idiomatic expressions. Spanish readers will understand your Argentine translator perfectly, but they will probably conclude it is a poor translation rather than a different dialect and won't hesitate to say so in a review.

This is another exception where the most widely accepted dialect might not be that of the most populous country. Spain has a population of about 46 million, which is much lower than Mexico's 122 million. Dialects also vary amongst South American and Latin American countries. While Spain holds little influence over its former colonies in everyday life, in literature at least, European Spanish seems to be the most universally accepted. Another interesting tidbit: at present the largest Spanish market for eBooks is neither Spain nor Mexico. It is the U.S. market on Amazon.com.

English

Large Market
 Popular genres: Romance, Mystery/Thriller, Science Fiction
 Popular online stores: Amazon.com, Amazon.co.uk, Kobobooks.com, Apple, Google Play
 Overview:

My books are written in English, so I do not translate them. I follow American spelling and grammar. My advice to non-English authors who want to translate into English is the same: focus on the preference of the country with the largest population, which is the United States. American English is understood by all English speakers even though there are variations. The American reader is the most critical and unforgiving and might give poor reviews when reading U.K. English or another English variation. Sometimes these differences in grammar and spelling are mistakenly assumed to be errors. There is nothing like a bad review to hurt book sales, so if you had to choose one, I recommend American.

Both the U.S. and the U.K. have a large supply of books, so price-points are low due to high competition and supply. But if you manage to hit a bestseller list, you can do very well.

Most traditionally published books that are translated into English will have both U.S. and U.K. versions since the U.K. is also a sizeable market. Smaller markets such as Canada, Australia, and New Zealand tend to follow variations on U.K. spelling.

You have probably noticed by now that the Romance genre seems to be the most popular genre in every country and language. Mystery and crime fiction is often a close second. For these genres, also make sure that your book's sub-genre is equally popular, especially within the romance genre since some heat levels will not be universally accepted everywhere.

Other languages

There are a few other languages that I am watching but am not quite ready to commit to just yet. These markets look promising but it is just too early to know whether they will be worthwhile or not. While they have potential in one or more areas, there also risks. Things can change quickly, so I will be ready to jump in should circumstances change.

Hindi

Large Market

At first glance, India represents a huge market; however there are significant issues you need to be aware of. While English is widely spoken and read as a second language by many, especially those with higher education, it is not still not understood at a reading level by a lot of people. English is usually secondary to a first language of Hindi or one of the many other native languages.

Even when English is understood, that doesn't mean that a person will want to read in their second language. It's a given that people prefer to read in their first language over any other. There are more than 22 languages and thousands of dialects spoken in India, so what at first appears to be a large market is actually a very fragmented one.

Also, a large proportion of the population is illiterate and piracy is widespread. Books are not affordable or even accessible for most people. Factor in extremely low prices and all the different dialects and the end result is low probability of profits—at least in Hindi.

English is another story. Most parents want their children to learn English to maximize career opportunities, so this is probably where the biggest growth opportunities lie. However, the bestselling books are nonfiction books for educational and career purposes.

Indians are receptive to reading on their smartphones, and eBooks are readily available. For the moment, at least, it might be better to focus on pricing strategies and increasing your sales channels for your English books in the Indian market rather than translating your books.

I also think audiobooks will grow to become more popular than eBooks in this market. I also believe that eBook subscription services will become the primary way to consume books in India. Time will tell, so I will wait to see what develops.

For all books no matter what the format, an even bigger roadblock to book sales in India is the absence of payment systems. Most Indians do not use credit cards. Noncash purchase payments are handled primarily through their mobile carrier accounts. There are several promising developments for payment systems, but until these are in place, this language isn't likely to pay off soon.

Indonesian

Large Market

Bahasa Indonesian is the official language of Indonesia, but there are more than 300 languages spoken, so what at first appears to be a huge market is a somewhat fragmented one. Disposable income is low too. This language is on my watch list, but it is not a priority.

Japanese

Large Market
    High Prices
    Low Competition

At present it is not that easy to distribute and sell books in Japan other than on Amazon Japan, so I am watching this language and waiting for new developments and opportunities. Rakuten, the parent company of Kobo, is the major Japanese e-commerce store and Amazon also has a store. The translation challenges relate more to finding a good Japanese translator. I haven't seen many translators that are native Japanese speakers yet. However, it is a market worth exploring, so it is a priority on my watch list.

Russian

Large Market

The Russian market is potentially very large, but there is rampant piracy and prices are low. At this point, I don't see enough potential to make a Russian translation worthwhile, but that could change quickly.

4

TRANSLATION OPTIONS

Before you begin looking for translators, you will want to have an idea of translation options available as well as potential costs and the various ways to pay for a translation.

Translation can be expensive, especially if you have many books you want to translate into one or more languages. Some authors aren't comfortable spending money up front for a translation when they don't know the local market or have the confidence or risk tolerance to undertake a translation in a language they don't understand.

Others prefer to pay for their translations outright to maintain control and maximize potential profits.

Selling or Assigning Your Rights

Authors who want to minimize their risks sometimes choose to sell their foreign rights, even if their untranslated books are indie published. For this arrangement, you would usually work through an agent, but foreign publishers sometimes contact authors directly if they are interested in translating a book. As you might guess, the author's potential income from this route will be lower if the book is successful, but the plus is that the author doesn't have to make an upfront investment and might even get an advance.

A more recent alternative is Amazon Crossing, where you can submit your books for consideration. If your book is chosen for a particular language, you will have no upfront costs and will earn royalties just as you would if you contracted with a publisher. Amazon Crossing translators bid for the work and are usually paid a flat fee plus a small royalty if a certain threshold of sales are achieved. The biggest advantage of going this route is the Amazon promotion machine and favored placement in the Amazon store.

Amazon Crossing translators are usually good and one thing to note is that these translators also do other freelance work, so you can always approach one directly if you are interested in working with them.

The disadvantage to both these approaches is that you give up control and part of the proceeds. The publisher gets the last word on cover choice and branding, and you will assign your rights for a very lengthy time, often the copyright term of life 70+ years. However, in comparison, the Amazon term is shorter at 10 years.

The advantage is that there is very little for you to do other than sign the contract.

Managing the Translation Process Yourself

There are also several ways to handle the translations yourself, which is my preference. There is some time investment upfront, but it is well worth the effort. There might also be a monetary investment depending on the method you choose. The most common methods are:

- Pay the translator a flat fee based on the length of the work, usually expressed as a cost per word
- Pay a royalty as a percentage of book earnings
- A combination of the above

I have done all three of these. My preference varies depending on the translator cost and the particular market. It's a bit of a judgment call as there are pros and cons to each, and some of those might be more significant factors in some markets than in others.

You will obviously choose the arrangement that works best for you, but whatever rate or royalty amount you settle on, try to think of the best result in terms of fairness for the translator too. Good translators are very hard to find, and considering everyone's interests and paying a fair rate is the best way to develop and sustain a productive and profitable long-term relationship.

Most importantly you want to incentivize the translator to do a good translation and make it worthwhile for her to work with you again on other books. I can't think of a better person to have on your side in a foreign market. Even if they are not marketers or promoters, they can help you navigate a foreign market. Most often they will promote your book without even realizing it, since they are publicizing their translation of your work as part of their portfolio.

A couple of my translators have helped me get into libraries in their home markets by approaching the libraries with my books. I never suggested or asked them to do that—they just did. I find that when you are fair in your business dealings, you often reap unexpected rewards. Aside from that, it's just good karma.

You have probably figured out by now that translation fees can quickly add up, especially if you have many books. You should also have several books translated and published in each language before you expect any substantial results. Just like the books in your original language, the more books you have, the more read-through and discoverability you potentially get. Expect to have two or three books out in a language before sales start to gain traction. Once that happens, you gain visibility and your earnings will grow.

More books translated means higher translation expenses, though. There are obviously many ways of financing your translations, but the following arrangements are the most common ways to work with a translator.

Flat fee

Under this arrangement, you pay the entire cost of the translation. The traditional payment is a per word amount, based on the word count in the original language. The rate per word varies by language and can vary due to supply and demand. If there are many translators but not enough translation work, the rates will likely be lower. Few translators but high demand usually results in a higher rate. Usually, you pay an initial deposit with the rest due upon handover of the final translation.

The cost will depend upon the going rate for that language globally as well as prevailing wage rates in the translator's country. At the time I wrote this book, German translations were in very high demand. Some of the better translators charge 10 to 15 Euro cents a word or more, which equates to $8,000-$12,000 for an 80,000-word novel. Some even ask for a percentage of royalties on top of this rate.

A popular language with many translators competing for work will have lower rates. Some translators work for rates as low as 2 cents per word, but that is the exception, not the norm. That doesn't mean that a less popular language will have a lower rate, though. In fact, the rate could be higher because there are fewer translators to choose from.

While the rates are dictated by the market, there are always translators who might be willing to work for lower rates in order to gain experience to establish themselves as literary translators. If you can do the necessary due diligence, you could find a great translator this way at a very reasonable cost.

Under the flat fee arrangement, the author bears all the risk. The translator gets paid when they provide the finished product, regardless of whether the book is successful or not. The author only recoups her investment if the book sells enough copies to offset the up-front cost. That is easier said than done, as it is difficult to sell and promote your book in a language you don't speak or understand.

The major advantage to paying a flat fee is that once you pay the translator, there is nothing further to do. No tedious accounting for royalty share payments is required, and there are no hard feelings from the translator if you lower the book's price, make it free, or otherwise impact a translator's royalties. They get paid no matter how the book performs. Many top-notch translators only work for a flat fee.

Many of the best translators will work for the high end of the flat fee (such as 15 cents a word in the German example), plus want a small percentage like 2-5% on sales. Personally, if I am paying this much, I won't agree to the percentage on top. I don't want the administrative hassle and also feel that a generous fee is more than enough.

This pay up-front method is straightforward and has the least amount of administrative burden since there is no need to consult a partner about pricing and no detailed royalty statements to produce.

It is the most expensive in terms of up-front cost but might be the cheapest option in the long run if your book takes off and becomes a bestseller. Study the selling prices in that language and genre and consider how many copies you will have to sell before you recover your costs. My rule is that if I can recover the cost outlay within 1-2 years, I pay up front.

Pros

- You own the translation outright. You are free to distribute to all sales channels or just one without consulting with the translator or impacting their earnings.
- You continue to hold exclusive derivative rights for other formats such as audiobooks, paperbacks, or other things like movie options, so you can immediately exploit these rights and earn more money faster.
- Pricing flexibility. You might choose to make the first book free or cheap for marketing purposes, something that would be unfair to your translator under a royalty share basis.
- Eliminates the need for the tedious record-keeping required under a royalty share agreement.

- Minimizes risk of legal disputes since the contract ends once the book is delivered.
- Might be the cheapest option for you if your book sells well.
- You will get your translation completed quickly since the translator will prioritize it as "paid" work rather than a royalty share with its longer payment timeframe and uncertainty.

Cons

- You bear the cost of the translation, which can be prohibitively expensive and add up if you have many books.
- You might never recoup your investment. Book prices can drop, subscription models changed, and competition could increase, preventing you from recovering your costs.
- Less incentive for an unethical translator to provide a quality product as there is no revenue at risk once the final product is delivered. You might not realize there are edit or quality issues until you get bad reviews.
- Translator might not be motivated to help you with marketing and promotion in the foreign market once they have been paid in full.

Royalty share

Direct agreement with translator

A royalty share is the least risky for the author in terms of cost. However, it bears the greatest risk for the translator, who typically works full-time for one to two months on a novel with no guarantees of success or payment. They don't know how much they will earn over time or even when they will earn it since their fee is a percentage of book sales. This is a departure from how translators have normally worked in the past, so not all translators are willing to work for a royalty share.

Translating a novel is a significant time investment for your translator and it is only fair that they have as much information as you do. It is always best to be upfront with your translator about estimated sales to the best of your ability so that they go into any translation with a realistic sense of their earnings potential and the risks involved.

Most people have an overly rosy view of publishing and author earnings in general. To avoid disappointment or unrealistic expectations, it is a good idea to provide your translator with high-level details of your current sales for the book and a rough range of earnings they could expect from a translation. Use your current net sales revenue and units sold with the proviso that results will vary in a foreign market.

Net sales revenue is particularly important since most translators have no idea what percentage of a book's list price actually accrues to the author. Provide lots of disclaimers of course, but be honest and up front. Provide broad ranges of earning estimates so that they at least have a sense of the payoff in order to make an informed decision.

If you have a good translator, you will want to establish an ongoing relationship with them, ideally to translate all of your books in a given series. It is better to give conservative sales estimates and surpass them than it is to disappoint. Often the same sales success in the English market will not repeat in other languages and markets, and they should be made aware of that also.

A good working relationship with your translator makes things easier for you. Working with one talented translator on a series of books is much easier than screening and hiring a new translator for each book.

Translators willing to do royalty share agreements usually also have day jobs to pay the bills. A novel done on a part-time basis could take 6 months or more to translate, and even then there is no guarantee that the translator will agree to translate other books in your series. Even if they do, it could take years to translate all of the books in the series. I think it is a good idea to keep the same translator for an entire series where possible. Just like the original author, they add their own "voice" to the translation. You will want it to be consistent across the same books in a series.

Most translators will not prefer this type of arrangement. Those open to it are either looking to gain literary translation experience or, if they already have experience, are taking a calculated risk that your book could be a breakout hit. If it is, the author will end up paying far more for the translation that if she had paid up front for it. Many translators will ask to read your book first in order to assess it. Consider this a sign of a good translator who is serious about their work.

If you contract directly with your translator, you will want to be careful about the agreement terms. A reasonable length of time is five years since most books earn the bulk of their revenue in the first couple of years.

Some authors decide to split royalties in perpetuity with their translators. I don't like this method as I don't want to be still calculating royalties on dozens or hundreds of translations when I'm 90 years old. If you are careful in choosing the book, the markets, and the translator, the translator should more than earn their fee in a five-year time period. If your book ends up being a bestseller, you can always decide to pay the translator an extra bonus.

One of the major drawbacks of a straight royalty share is that the translator has nothing at risk if they fail to meet deadlines or decide to quit halfway through your project. Many authors have complained of never hearing from a translator again after the translation sample was approved. You can always start over with another translator, but in the meantime, you have delayed your translation timeline by months or even years. If you have a series to translate, delays in the first book can hold up the whole series.

One science fiction author I know had contracted with a well-known and talented German translator to translate his book, the first in a seven book sci-fi series, in a 60-day timeframe. That time was suggested by the translator, not the author. Unfortunately, that was two years ago, and the author is still waiting for his book.

Technically the translator has breached the contract. The translator claims the book is 80% finished and, since it is a royalty share arrangement with a translator he could otherwise not afford, the author is reluctant to take action. He keeps hoping for the book that never comes. I'm not sure what I would do in the same situation.

The following summarizes the pros and cons dealing directly with the translator.

Pros

- No upfront translation cost for the author.
- Translator is motivated to provide a quality translation.
- Translator is incentivized to assist you with marketing and promotion of the book in the foreign market since this potentially increases their earnings over the agreement term.

Cons

- Less pricing flexibility, such as offering perma-free books or discounts, without discussion and agreement from your translator.
- Record-keeping can be time-consuming and tedious since you will need to track sales by book, country, currency, and platform.
- Depending on the country, there could be international tax issues such as withholding payments, exemptions or unexpected tax liabilities.
- You might expose yourself to foreign currency losses if you are paid in one currency and must pay the translator in another.

- The translator might miss deadlines or not deliver. Not only does this impact the current book, but also subsequent books in the series. The translator has no monetary incentive to deliver if they are busy with something else.

You can also do a variation of this method by working under a royalty share arrangement with the translator on a translation platform like Babelcube rather than dealing directly with that person. In addition to the pros and cons above, there are some additional considerations if you decide to go this route.

Royalty Share Using a Translation Platform

In the next chapter we will get into the nuts and bolts of using third-party platforms, but for now we will just look at what to consider when deciding whether or not to go this route.

The best thing about translation platforms is that they take care of all the administrative tasks. The translation platform will also intercede on your behalf in the case of non-performance, reminding translators to meet deadlines and dealing with other non-performance issues, such as disputes about the translation quality itself. Instances of this are rare, but they do happen. Personally, I don't like to deal with such matters, so I find this arrangement to be a huge plus.

There are also legal benefits to this arrangement since the translation platform has a standard contract with terms that will protect your intellectual property rights, such as the German copyright ownership issue mentioned earlier.

This is precisely what they do in Babelcube's version of a "work for hire" contract. I could easily incorporate the same terms into my contracts, but since I'm not a lawyer, I hesitate to do this. Whatever platform you use, read the contract carefully and ensure everything is clearly stated so there are no misunderstandings later.

We will discuss specific platforms in the next chapter.

To summarize, a translation through a translation platform is an attractive option with no upfront investment by the author. The only significant risk is a poor translation which you can avoid by carefully choosing your translator and evaluating the sample translation.

Pros

- The translation platform deals with the record-keeping, payments, and taxes.
- The translation platform can intercede on your behalf if there are contract issues such as late delivery or non-performance.
- Work for hire contracts protect your intellectual property rights.
- Once the term is up, you get all subsequent royalties and can exploit your intellectual rights.
- Very cost effective and low risk.

Cons

- The translation platform takes a percentage of net revenue, leaving less money to split between you and the translator.
- You cannot exploit your subsidiary rights, such as audiobooks that are based on the translation, until the contract term is over.
- There is a middleman between you and the published books, limiting your ability to set prices and categories, and use platform-specific advertising programs to directly promote your books on some sales platforms.

Specific platforms will be discussed in detail in the next chapter.

Hybrid Flat Fee + Royalty share

A flat fee plus a royalty share can be an effective compromise. It provides your translator with some certainty with a guaranteed base amount plus an added incentive if the book does well. It encourages the translator to promote and market the book to earn even more. If you want a translator to help you with promotion, make sure you also include the specifics in the contract with clear deliverables, such as translating sales copy, posting articles, etc.

A hybrid arrangement like this can also keep things on track since the contractor will not get paid the lump sum until they provide the translated book. Typically the lump sum will be at least half of what it would be under a flat fee arrangement, though it can vary to whatever you agree upon with your translator.

This hybrid arrangement can be more complicated for you, the author, because it has all the complexities of a royalty share agreement in terms of record-keeping without much benefit to you. One advantage is that it could attract more experienced and talented translators.

A variation of this arrangement is an option offered by a new third-party translation platform. The author can augment the translator's royalty share arrangement with a lump sum that is provided upon completion of the translation. More about this platform in the next chapter.

Pros

- You can attract more experienced translators at a lower up-front cost.
- You pay less money up front.
- You provide the translator with a greater incentive to deliver a quality product within the deadline since their revenue is at risk from both a timing and performance point of view (if it is a poor translation, it won't sell).

Cons

- Less pricing flexibility, such as offering perma-free books or discounts, without discussion and agreement from your translator.
- Record-keeping can be time-consuming and tedious since you will need to track sales by book, country, currency, and platform.
- Depending on the country, there could be international tax issues such as tax withholding payments, exemptions, or unexpected tax liabilities.
- You might expose yourself to foreign currency losses if you are paid in one currency and must pay the translator in another.
- Unless specifically exempted in the contract, you cannot exploit your subsidiary rights, such as audiobooks that are based on the translation, until the contract term is over.
- You might never recover your initial investment. Book prices can drop, subscription models can change, and competition can increase, preventing you from recouping your costs.

Selling Your Foreign Rights

There is one last option, which is selling your foreign rights. You can do this regardless of whether you publish yourself or through a publisher. Some authors prefer this option, thinking that their foreign translation earnings will be minimal and that the small return is not worthy of a huge investment in time.

There is nothing wrong with this approach, but sometimes it becomes a self-fulfilling prophecy. Under this option, you must pay an agent a percentage to find a foreign publisher, and the publisher will want to make a profit. It is difficult to know how much money you could have potentially earned once you go this route. But you can see how earnings can shrink quickly with more people in the pipeline!

There are always situations where this makes sense. Examples are markets that you couldn't reach on your own directly or through an intermediary, or where it would be too time-consuming or expensive.

Market barriers are coming down all the time, though, so keep this important consideration in mind. You don't want to sell your rights for decades or possibly your lifetime, only to find out later that the previously impossible is now possible and easy to do. If in doubt, wait and see how things develop. Waiting it out is much easier than making decisions that cannot be reversed, only to regret them later.

Pros

- Nothing further for you to do, so you can spend more time writing.
- The publisher has expertise in the foreign market, so in theory, at least, they can market the book better than you can.
- Local publishers have established distribution channels. It is easier for them to get your translated books exposure and into bookstores and libraries.
- No outlay of money.

Cons

- You lose control on how rights are monetized, if at all.
- Rights are unlikely to ever be reverted back to you, even if the book doesn't sell.
- The agreement will likely last for at least your lifetime, so there is no turning back.
- You will earn less overall, since you have to split any proceeds with your agent, the foreign publisher, and any other parties involved.
- You will have no control over the cover, pricing, categorization, promotion, and so on.

Now that you have an overview of the potential costs of translations and the various ways to pay for them, you probably have some preliminary conclusions of what method will work best for you and your books. In the next chapter, we will look at where to find translators as well as some of the most popular third-party translation platforms.

5

HOW AND WHERE TO START

Where to Find Literary Translators

You can find translators in a number of places, including translation websites, freelance websites, through author referrals and online platforms specifically designed for translations. We'll discuss how to evaluate them in a later chapter, but for now let's just look at where to find them.

We'll look at the translation platforms first. I think this is the easiest way for the beginner to start. They operate like a literary dating site where authors and translators meet. In the simplest terms, a translator picks one of your books to translate and makes an offer, or you choose a translator and ask them if they would be interested in translating your book. In return, you share the proceeds with the translator and also with the translation platform for the term of the agreement, which is usually 5 years.

Translation Platforms

Translation platform websites provide all the administrative functionality including publishing and distribution, a source to find translators, contracts and dispute resolution, sales tracking and payment.

Net royalties received are then divided amongst the author, translator, and the translation platform.

This is the easiest way to start translations, but the downside is that you must give up some of your fees and you might also lose some control in product pricing, distribution, categorization, and promotional opportunities.

The math part is easy: if you expect to pay the platform more in fees than you would a translator, then dealing directly with a translator is for you. Pricing is the biggest issue for me, since most of these platforms don't allow for regional pricing, at least not yet. This is a huge disadvantage, since I want my Spanish book to be priced lower for the Mexican marketplace and higher for the U.S. and Spain.

Pricing also impacts promotion, since many retailers, such as Kobo and Apple, want prices to end in 0.99. Merchandisers at these stores have told me that they won't consider books for promotional or merchandising opportunities if the list price ends in 0.74 or something else other than 0.99.

Currently, the major translation platforms only have one field for a selling price in U.S. dollars. Prices in non-U.S. markets are simply the U.S. price multiplied by the foreign exchange rate, so weird prices ending in something other than .99 are unavoidable. Hopefully the translation platforms will add geographical pricing functionality to address this deficiency. Until then, it can impact discoverability and potential sales in many markets.

Another disadvantage is categorization. Each retailer has slightly different categories, and I want my books to be in the most suitable category with the least amount of competition to maximize discoverability. Even choosing the best categories for the biggest sales channel does not guarantee that they will actually be categorized there by the time they reach the various retailers. I find that the books often end up in large general categories like "mystery", rather than the targeted subcategory I had chosen.

The main translation platforms available today include:

Babelcube.com – based in the U.S.

Fiberead.com – based in China

Traduzione Libri – based in Italy

They all operate on the same basic royalty share model, where the author pays nothing up front but surrenders a portion of royalties over the contract term.

Babelcube

Babelcube.com is the most established of the royalty-share translation platforms and the one I recommend starting with. Their platform is well-designed and easy to use. The exclusivity term is 5 years, after which you are free to publish directly yourself and exercise any derivative rights such as creating audio books that are based on the translation.

Royalties are shared between the translator, author, and Babelcube, with percentages that vary as sales thresholds are reached. The initial sales thresholds favor the translator, which switches to the author earning a higher percentage once higher sales are attained.

You load your book covers and blurbs first and then search for translators in a number of languages by choosing certain criteria and adding your own with search terms. Translators can also search for authors in a similar fashion and choose one for your books to translate. They then make you an offer by providing a sample translation for you to evaluate.

I recommend actively searching for translators rather than waiting for a translator to make an offer. Many of the good translators are booked out 6 months to a year or more, so you can at least get on their waiting list if they are interested in translating your books.

You are allowed to make one offer per day for each book, and it can take days or even months for translators to respond! For this reason, I recommend using a spreadsheet with tabs for each language to track who you have contacted with the date. It can get confusing if you have many books, since the only other way is to scroll through all your messages on the platform, and messages aren't sorted by language.

I have developed a strategy of prioritizing the languages I wanted translated first and then made a list of all translators that met my criteria. If you have a series and you want a single translator to do the entire series, remember that each book can take 6 months or more to translate, If you are already waiting 6 months to work with them, then that's a 1-year wait just for book one.

Translators on Babelcube run the gamut from experienced literary translators with Master's degrees, recent translation grads looking to gain experience, unemployed and retired bilingual people trying something new, and everything in between.

There are some excellent translators on Babelcube, but there are also a lot of people with no translation experience whatsoever. It is a worthwhile investment to spend some time carefully checking a translator's experience and suitability before committing to work with them. More on that in a later chapter.

As of this writing, the languages offered on Babelcube include the following:

Afrikaans
Dutch
English
French
German
Italian
Japanese
Norwegian
Portuguese
Spanish

Babelcube says that it only offers languages where there is a good supply of translators and adequate demand from authors. I have found this to be true in most cases. However, there are very few translators for both Japanese and Norwegian, and little to no distribution channels that go to Japanese or Norwegian stores. There are some additional languages that I would like to see added but haven't been as of yet.

The platform itself is simple to use and reasonably well-designed. Where it is less satisfactory is customer service and publishing speed. Queries often go unanswered, which can be incredibly frustrating if you are having issues.

Babelcube appears to be suffering from growing pains and has only a few employees who are spread thin. There are technological issues at times too. Messages between authors and translators sometimes do not get delivered. Publishing can take a long time and there can be significant delays with no explanation. An eBook could be published on Apple but not published on Amazon until weeks or even months later, for example. At least this was the case in late 2016. I understand the platform had a technology issue, so I hope this has been permanently resolved. As you can imagine, this can make promoting a new release extremely difficult.

Authors and translators alike complain about Babelcube's service levels, which certainly need to improve if they want to remain competitive as new translation platforms enter the market. Their platform is well-designed but poorly implemented. If they made some improvements on the execution side it could be great.

As far as the translation itself, you can choose to work with a single translator or a team of two translators. I recommend using "translator teams" wherever possible. This consists of a main translator and a second one who proofreads. This not only minimizes errors but it increases the odds that the translation will stay on track.

If a translator hasn't indicated in their profile that they work on a translator team basis, I always ask them if they will. This means that they will have to share a portion of their payments with the second translator, but it benefits them too. They will finish the translation faster and a second person will do the editing portion. You will get a more polished book.

Babelcube operates on a royalty-share basis. The royalties are on a sliding scale, with the translators earning 55% of net receipts for the first $2,000 USD, dropping to 10% of net receipts for sales over $8000 USD. The author's share is 30% for the first $2,000 USD, rising to 75% over $8000 USD during the 5-year term. You can see a chart here: http://www.babelcube.com/faq/revenue-share

One thing to note is that translators seem to prefer short stories because of the royalty levels. What they don't realize is that short stories don't sell nearly as much as longer works like novels, so it doesn't work in their favor as much as they think it does.

How it works

- Authors upload their books to the Babelcube platform.
- Authors can search for translators and translators can search for books to translate.
- Translators make "an offer" to translate a book by contacting the author and providing a short sample in the timeframe.
- Once the author accepts the translation sample, a larger sample is done and then the standard royalty share contract is entered into.
- Translators can work alone or with another translator as editor and proofreader.
- Authors are paid via Paypal (the only payment method at present).

Fiberead

Fiberead.com is a Chinese translation platform that translates into Simplified Chinese and Traditional Chinese, offering the author 30% of net royalties. They plan to offer other languages in the future. Fiberead represents a significant opportunity for Indie authors to get their books onto all the major platforms in China. However, there are also some serious drawbacks, so proceed with caution.

On the plus side, Fiberead is less self-service than Babelcube. It operates more like a publisher in that once you upload your books, everything else is overseen by the Fiberead project manager. A team of translators is assigned to translate, edit, and proofread the book. Expect lots of questions from your translators about your text as each translator, editor, and proofreader will have their own questions.

I have done several translations with Fiberead and the process seems thorough with a well-designed and implemented platform. Fiberead also takes care of the publishing, distribution, and pricing steps. The author doesn't do anything further once the book is uploaded to the Fiberead site.

Fiberead also has very good distribution channels to all the major Chinese stores—stores that are difficult or impossible to get into from outside China. However, there are some issues I have with Fiberead as a company. Fiberead recently changed some of its contract terms, and some of the clauses they added are quite disadvantageous to the author. My books were published under an earlier version of the contract prior to these changes. I don't plan to translate any more books with Fiberead unless they change their current contract.

I caution you to read the agreement carefully and not proceed unless you fully understand the contract language. In particular, note the derivative rights clause, which assigns your rights to Fiberead. The contract allows them to further develop other derivative intellectual property from your story. In other words, it is a rights grab.

Under this clause, you are essentially granting them permission to sell movie, game, and all other rights without any further input or approval from you. Some authors are fully aware of this clause but reason that they wouldn't be able to monetize these rights otherwise. But you never know what will happen tomorrow, and there certainly could be other Chinese publishers willing to offer you better terms.

If your book is not popular, you have probably lost nothing, but if sales start to spike, you will wish you had retained those rights to exercise later. China is a huge market and not one where you want to make a mistake.

Other Fiberead clauses mention the author paying for paperback expenses, something they seemed to have backed away from slightly after criticism. Asking the author to pay for printing expenses when they have already given up 70 percent of net revenues to Fiberead and the Fiberead translators is unfair. Their terms certainly aren't competitive with other translation platforms, but maybe it's because they don't have any real competition at present.

And, sadly, many authors just sign the contract without reading it.

Last but not least, Fiberead refuses to give authors a copy of their translated work in ePub or any other format, saying that they don't distribute copies in order to avoid piracy. It makes no sense to me that an author would pirate their own products, and providing a copy is common business practice. Many authors have complained to Fiberead about this but to no avail.

I am confident that more competition and better terms for Chinese translations will emerge in the very near future. In the meantime, I would suggest holding off on any translations with Fiberead until it amends its contract terms to something more commercially acceptable.

How it works

- Authors upload their books to the Fiberead platform.
- Each book is assigned a project manager who oversees the entire translation and publishing process.
- Translators bid on books, are graded on a translation sample and, if successful, work in a team made up of translators, editors, and proofreaders.
- Fiberead does everything from choosing the translators, publishing, setting prices, and choosing categories.
- Authors are paid via Paypal (the only payment method at present).

Traduzione Libri

Traduzionelibri.it is a brand new royalty-share platform operated by an Italian company called Tektime. There are some languages such as Polish and Arabic available on this platform that are not currently available on Babelcube. This is great news—until you realize that many of the languages they offer have no distribution channels in that language. Since you can't distribute or upload the translation anywhere else for the term of the contract, this is—for the moment at least--a show-stopper. I hope this limitation will be resolved soon, but at the moment it is difficult to see sales grow quickly.

The platform offers a bigger initial royalty share to the translator than Babelcube does, so it might be easier to get translators under a royalty share model since the potential earnings are better. The platform operates just like Babelcube, including the 5-year contract period.

However, the platform is very new and unproven, only a few months old at the time of this writing. The site is in Italian with an English translation (see bottom of website) and while it is functional, it is obvious that they are still working out some of the website kinks. If distribution channels can be found for all the languages it offers, then it will be welcome competition to Babelcube.

As of this writing, the languages offered on Traduzione Libri include the following:

Esperanto
Afrikaans
Malaysian
Norwegian
Polish
Romanian
Russian
Arabic
Sinhala
Slovak
Swedish
Thai
Turkish
Spanish
Albanian
Macedonian
Serbian
Croatian

Burmese
Hungarian
French
Bulgarian
German
Czech
Danish
Italian
Dutch
Estonian
Finnish
Portuguese
Greek
Japanese
Icelandic
Indonesian
Chinese

I am at a loss as to how and where I might monetize an Esperanto translation, but you never know when markets might take off.

How it works

- Authors upload their books to the Traduzione Libri platform.
- Translators place offers on your books and provide a translation sample for you to evaluate.
- Authors can supplement the royalty percentage with an optional flat fee payable upon delivery of the translation.

Other Translator Websites

If you decide that the translation royalty share platforms are not for you and you would rather deal more directly with translators, there are plenty of places to find them. It is rare but not impossible that you will find any translator willing to do a royalty share arrangement.

Here are some common sites to find a translator:

Translator-specific sites

Proz.com

This website is especially for translation, whether literary or not. It is the largest global translator network, and most translators with formal training and/or professional experience will most likely have a profile here. You can post a translation job or search for translators to contact. You can also look up a translator to check out their experience and ratings by previous customers. You might also want to search for translators here using your own specific criteria as a starting point since you can find their websites and contact info here. It is also a good place to get a sense of the going rates in each particular language. I'll help you with developing translator evaluation criteria in a later chapter. For now, let's just look at the sites and what they offer.

Translator's Café is another site similar to Proz.

General freelancer sites

You can also find translators through freelancer websites such as Upwork (formerly Elance), though you should be aware that the website usually takes a significant cut out of the total fee. That means the translators have to increase their prices to cover the fee, or else work for less money. The best translators with a portfolio of work generally don't work for less money, so in some cases, you are better off contracting with them directly.

These sites utilize rating systems for both buyer and seller so that both are incentivized to act as good business partners.

Some advantages of going through a freelancer website are similar to those of the royalty-share translation platforms. You have a third party dealing with payments or disputes. If something does go wrong, the translator still has a vested interest in delivering as contracted if they want a good rating and continued work on the site.

Another place I haven't tried but is used by some authors is Fiverr. I wouldn't recommend this avenue since the whole premise of the site is small 5-dollar gigs. You won't find many, or maybe even any, professionally qualified translators here. The translation on this site is more geared towards things like translating a letter, not something as complex as a novel.

I've also heard of authors finding translators on Craigslist, often at very favorable rates. While I don't question this website as a place to find freelancers of any type, I'm much more comfortable sourcing translators at the specialized places translators tend to hang out.

Referrals and recommendations

You can also find translators through referrals and recommendations from other authors. Just keep in mind that everyone's standards differ, so someone's excellent rating might not be to the same standard as yours. Also remember that many people will avoid giving bad references because even if they are not satisfied, they don't want to hurt a translator's chance of future work, or they don't want a bad reference getting traced back to them.

No matter how good the reference, be sure to still get a sample of the translator's work and have it evaluated, preferably by another professional translator. At the very least, have it evaluated by a native speaker who likes to read your genre and lives or has lived recently in the same country as the destination language.

Direct contract with translator

If you do find a good literary translator who comes well-recommended with excellent references from other authors, you might want to deal directly with them. Or maybe you have already done a translation with them on Babelcube or another platform and decide to work with them directly on the next translation. I have done the latter several times. It's quite common to start out on a translation platform and as you get comfortable with one another, mutually decide to work directly with each other off-platform on your next project.

If you deal directly, you need to have the following in place:

- A contract with similar terms specifying all the details including legal jurisdiction of the contract, who owns the rights (a "work for hire" in the legalese for the country of the contract), payment terms, and key dates (see translation contracts on the translation platform websites for examples)
- Any tax issues (payments, withholdings, reporting, and so on) are addressed for both your country and the translator's

Fees, payments, and timing

You can decide to pay a flat fee, royalty only, or some combination of the two. Since record-keeping can quickly become onerous if paying royalties to multiple translators, set up payment frequency to be no more frequently than quarterly.

Also ensure that your contract specifies a payment date that occurs *after* you have received your money. For example, paying a translator 30 days after the sale date wouldn't work very well because Amazon pays you 60 days after the month end in which the sales occur. You would be paying the translator with money you haven't actually received yet. Also, any transaction fees will likely be higher with many frequent payments than a few larger ones.

If you decide to pay a flat fee or per word rate, rates vary widely, so check any quoted rates against the going market rate for that language since the translator's rate depends on the language and supply/demand for the translation services in that market, the translator's experience, and the general wage levels in that country. You can get a sense of the rates on proz.com.

Translators typically charge by the word, from as low as $0.02 cents per word to $0.15 or higher. For an 80,000 word novel, this equates to a range of $1,600 to $12,000 per novel. That's quite a range and a significant investment, which is why I recommend not only checking market rates, but also trying the royalty share option first to get a good sense of how things work.

While I started with the royalty share arrangement, many of my translations have since been done on a flat fee basis. It really depends on several factors. If there is high demand for literary translators in a given language, they might have lots of work on a per word basis and not be willing to work for a royalty share.

My preference is to do the royalty share directly with the translator. This leaves more money to split with the translator and gives me more control over the book in terms of pricing and other things. It also incents the translator to help with whatever is needed to make the book a success. They don't have to do much, but it's much easier to ask a translator to help translate some marketing copy when you still have an ongoing relationship with them through the royalty payments.

Please beware though, that a direct arrangement can have significant pitfalls. If the translator doesn't deliver, or delivers a poor product, you have fewer options. Another downside is the amount of record-keeping involved. You will have to record and remit royalties to each translator, which can quickly become a lot of work if you are using multiple translators.

Finally, one often overlooked reason to consider a direct arrangement is if you want to put the book in Amazon's exclusive program, KDP Select. You can't do this with a translation on Babelcube or any other platform, since your book is automatically distributed to dozens of stores aside from Amazon, and there is no way to opt out.

Whatever payment arrangement you choose, my recommendation is to start small and get one book or short story done before you commit yourself to one direction.

6
WHAT DOES A TRANSLATOR DO EXACTLY?

A good translator is a bridge between worlds. They shape our words into a new language, translating and transforming our story into a new language while never losing the original meaning. Through my translators—and translations—I feel globally connected in ways I never did before.

Translating from one language to another sounds like something any bilingual person could do, right? Not quite. Translating a novel is not as simple as relaying information in another language. A good translator retains all of the passion in a romance and all of the tension in a thriller by capturing the words and voice of the author as well as a genre-specific writing style. In reality, it is much harder than it looks. They start with your book and rewrite it in a new language, keeping intact the author voice, style, and intent. The reader of the translated book enjoys the same reading experience as if they had read the story in the original language.

Just as many of your friends are completely fluent in English, few to none of them can write a book. You want both writing and language capabilities in a literary translator. The translator has not only a great command of both languages but also understands literature. Just because somebody knows what you mean does not guarantee that they will interpret and impart your words, voice, and emotion the same way to a different audience. Translation is similar to many professions in that we often only see the surface 5% of what a person does and not the other 95%.

Many translators will read your book first, cover to cover, before even deciding to translate it. Once they take it on, they will do several drafts. First, a draft to get everything down on paper, so to speak. After they have completed the first draft, they might take a break from the translation and let it rest a bit. Then they do several more drafts before the book is done. It's kind of like writing a novel, isn't it?

In fact, that's pretty much what they are doing, except you have already given them the plot, characters, and pacing to work with. A good translator will retain your voice and narrative style. Some translators are so good that they can make the translated version even better than the original book.

There are annual literary translation awards, including the Man Booker International prize, for best translated book. The best translators are sought-after and understandably command high fees for their work. These translators are probably beyond our budgets, but they all started somewhere. There are plenty of good literary translators at a reasonable cost in this highly-specialized field. Maybe one of them is a future Man Booker International winner in waiting.

Many experienced translators are looking to break into literary translation and are willing to work for less in order to gain experience. Lots of new translators are probably avid readers in your genre and make up for their inexperience with an intuitive sense of what works for your particular book.

On the flip side, choosing the wrong translator can have a lasting impact on your career as an author. A bad translation is something you could be stuck with forever, so it is critical to do your research. A poor translation is a reflection on you and your author brand. It is very difficult to undo so you want to get it right. A disappointed reader will not go on to read your other books. Even worse, they might tell other people not to either.

It also takes time for a translator to produce a quality translation.

Translations are expensive and for good reason. There is a lot of time and effort involved. However, there are always translators looking to gain experience in the growing literary translation field, and they can be flexible in terms of compensation. You can find arrangements that are mutually beneficial for both of you.

However, you also want to be upfront with your prospective translator about your book's earnings potential, especially if you plan to do a royalty-share arrangement with them. Unit sales can be misleading, especially if they were free downloads or 99-cent sales. Try to give the translator an estimate of your source language (English, in my case) revenue earned and let them use that as a starting point for comparison.

Many people, including translators, operate under the assumption that best-selling books are guaranteed to sell well in other languages. It certainly increases the odds, but nothing is guaranteed. While popular books bring in a lot of revenue, it doesn't always happen in a short period of time either. You can provide broad estimates of your expectations, but be up-front with your translator about what to expect in terms of both dollars and timing.

And it goes without saying that sales are dependent upon the quality of the translation itself.

Once you find a good translator, you will want to establish a long-term partnership and work on future books together. Just as important is ensuring that you have good communication channels with a translator. A lack of any communication at all can be a warning sign that all is not well.

I had a bad first experience with a translator who had initially provided me with a very good sample. I went ahead and signed a contract with her, but she missed multiple deadlines and didn't answer my emails for months on end. When she did answer, she gave a multitude of excuses, and things just weren't progressing. While I tried to be flexible, I felt uneasy about her lack of communication and evasiveness.

I don't mind minor delays because I understand that most translators have day jobs. Life gets in the way sometimes. The most important thing to me is a quality translation that is not rushed. But this translator misled me, so I started to wonder about the actual translation itself.

I had done everything right in terms of checking the translator's background and other reviews and even had references from other authors. This translator came highly recommended by another author who had translated numerous books with her, so I wanted to be understanding about her circumstances.

But months went by and deadlines were missed multiple times. My gut told me that the translation wasn't going to happen. I had exhausted all of my options, other than breaking the contract. I didn't want to do this, so I asked her to send me the text she had translated so far, and after several excuses and delays, she finally did. I was shocked to discover that she had used Google Translate for the rest of the book, something that would have immediately earned the book multiple 1-star reviews and angered readers.

To this day I don't understand why she did this, since under our 5-year royalty share deal she stood to lose from a poor translation just like I did. Of course, I would lose bigger because my rights would have been tied up with her for 5 years. Not only would I lose readers, but I would be unable to publish my book anywhere else until the contract was up. My reputation as an author in that language would be harmed and the book would get bad reviews. Luckily I was able to successfully terminate the contract without legal action. While I could have sued her for breach of contract, I'd rather invest that time and energy somewhere else, like writing my next book.

I learned a valuable lesson in that things can go wrong even with someone who comes highly recommended, and that it's never a bad idea to go with your gut. For whatever reason, my translator hadn't performed at the same level of quality for me as she had for the author who had recommended her. Past results aren't always a guarantee of future results, so be sure to always get your own independent evaluations of translation samples, regardless of glowing recommendations.

In the next chapter we will look at how to choose and evaluate a translator to ensure you don't make the same mistake I did.

7

HOW TO CHOOSE AND EVALUATE A TRANSLATOR

Following a few simple guidelines can quickly narrow down your choices to the most qualified people so you can start translating.

Communication is key

It's vitally important to establish a good rapport with your translator. After all, their interpretation will make or break your story. In addition to their technical qualifications and working style, you'll want to have open and honest communication, and be aligned on the frequency and type of communications throughout the process. Do you want someone who will check in with you periodically with questions, or someone who will complete the entire project independently? There is no right or wrong answer but you can avoid misunderstandings if you each have similar expectations about the process from the outset.

Native Speaker

As mentioned earlier, translators refer to the language they translate into as the *target language*. Your original book is considered the *source language*.

It goes without saying that the translator should be fluent in the source language. Ideally your translator will be a native speaker in the target language, with very few exceptions. They should also be resident in the country of the target language or have lived there within the last 5-10 years. Languages are always changing, and phrases go in and out of style. You don't want your book to use dated prose because the translator hasn't lived in the country for 30 years.

Also beware of someone who lists fluency in many languages. While they might have a high degree of fluency in all of them, there are probably only one or perhaps two that are at a high enough level of proficiency for a good literary translation.

Native Speakers vs. Fluent Non-Native Speakers

While you probably know people who are completely fluent in your language, if they are not native speakers, then you have probably noticed that there might be idiomatic expressions or words they are unfamiliar with or don't commonly use. This isn't an issue in everyday life and business, but literature is often nuanced in a way that only a native speaker will grasp.

This is not to say that there aren't translators with German as a second language that will give you an excellent translation; only that they are few and far between. Normally the exceptions are those who grew up in a completely bilingual home and school. You can certainly go with a non-native speaker, but you will have to take extra care in ensuring that their grasp of the language is at a very high level. Since I don't have the skills to do that kind of evaluation, I just stick to native speakers.

This is particularly true for fiction. In addition to translating your story into another language, the translator is also capturing the essence and tone of the story, as well as pacing and genre. If you write romance, you will want to find a translator familiar with the genre. You want the translator to capture not just the words but also the emotional journey and romantic tension between the characters. Ideally she would be an avid romance reader so that she will appreciate your particular word choices, pacing, and tone, and replicate those in her word choices and sentence structure. You want the translator to "get" your story. You want a native German speaker who is reading your German translation to enjoy the same experience as an English reader did with the English version.

Technical Qualifications

Translator qualifications vary widely by country. Some have standard qualifications and tests, and many countries offer advanced university degrees in translation. I typically look for a Master's degree in literary translation or its equivalent.

Literary translation is an art and requires the same creative touch that writing a book does. I suspect it might even be harder in some respects since a translator must stay within the boundaries the author has set while recreating that world so that it conveys the same emotion and feeling in a foreign culture and language. The translator is the bridge between two worlds.

I find that the qualifications are a good starting point, but just as there are many types of writers, there are also many types of translators. Translators might specialize in legal documents, medical transcription, and other areas unrelated to the literary world. However, the most technically proficient translator might not always be the best choice for your novel. You need a balance between technical proficiency and literary capability. Translators who read in your genre can be good finds.

Fluency in more than one language is still no guarantee that they will interpret your words with the same intent and emotion. As one author found out, her novel translation into Spanish was technically perfect. However, it lacked the same suspense and intensity because the words the translator used weren't quite what she would have chosen.

For instance, "he gulped water" changed into "he drank water" and "she sprinted down the alley" became "she ran down the road." While the first translation in each example is technically correct, it is certainly less exciting. In a thriller, this could be the difference between racing through an edge-of-your-seat thriller to not even turning the page.

It is vital that the translator understands the nuances of your word choices because he or she is essentially rewriting your book for a new audience.

Of course, there are always exceptions to the rules. In fact, two of my best translators have none of the above qualifications. Both have no formal translator qualifications but happen to be authors themselves. Neither write in my genre, but as writers, they understand my genre and the nuances of word choices typical to each genre. It is unusual to find completely bilingual authors who are also translators, but there are a few around.

Another advantage to an author-translator is that they will likely also be social media savvy and connected in your genre, or at least be knowledgeable about the book market and promotional opportunities in their language and country. They can be important allies in marketing your work. More about that later.

How to evaluate

You don't speak or read a word of German, so how can you possibly evaluate the quality of a German translation? Fortunately, there are several easy ways to narrow your list down to a few translators. The evaluation process can be a little time-consuming, but it is well worth the effort to find a good translator. You will hopefully develop an ongoing relationship with your translator and work on many more books together.

The evaluation starts before you even get a sample from the translator. Screening is of the utmost importance, and it is the reason why I like to choose my translators rather than waiting for them to make offers to translate my book. By applying some screening criteria, I can probably rule out 98% of the translators listed on a site like Babelcube. It requires a little effort but is well worth it because there are some real gems there too.

Screening

The Translator's Bio

Wherever you find your translator, he or she has probably provided a short biographical blurb in the source (my) language. I read the blurb, looking for the qualifications I mentioned earlier, but also looking for any issues in the spelling or grammar.

If there are any mistakes, they are either not completely fluent in the source language, or they wrote their blurb in a hurry. Whichever it is, I immediately rule them out because I don't want to end up with the same end result in my book due to either lack of fluency or lack of attention to detail.

You might also notice phrases that represent the correct sentence structure in the destination language but appear a little "off" in the source language, which in my case is English. The sentence just looks a little different...maybe even charming in another context.

My first instinct would be to forgive these differences in English since they will be correct in the destination language. But a fluently bilingual professional translator will adjust for these idiosyncrasies, so anyone who does not should make you hesitate. Did they fully understand the nuances in the original text? Remember, you only are looking at a short blurb. What is the chance that there will be something translated incorrectly in an entire novel?

They might produce a wonderful translation, but if they are not 100% proficient in the book's source language, there is always a chance that they could misunderstand or mistranslate something. Even if it's a small chance, I don't want to risk it.

Translator Credentials

Translators usually work in one or more language pairs and are ideally fluent in the first (source) language and native speakers of the second (destination) language. The source and destination language expressed together is known as the language pair.

Normally a translator will express their language pairs in abbreviated form. A translator that translates English into German (Deutsch) will express the language pair as EN-DE, which uses the ISO 639-2 standard language codes.

There are also many types of translators. You will want to use a literary translator where possible because they have specialized training in translation as well as literature. The training varies from country to country, but the gold standard is a Master's degree in literary translation. If they have experience working for a publishing house, even better, because they will be experienced with publishing standards and perhaps will have already translated many books.

Some countries have translator qualifications. For example, in Brazil, ABRATES – the Brazilian Association of Translators, awards national accreditation to a translator once they pass a proficiency test. In the United States, your translator might be a member of the ATA – American Translators Association. This provides assurance of a certain basic standard of technical ability since the translator has passed certain tests. It is a base level evaluation of competence, so use it as a starting point in your screening process.

While credentials and experience are no guarantee of a quality translation, some professional standing means that the translator has just as much credibility risk as you do. They won't want a bad review to tarnish their reputation and drive away business.

Professional translators usually have online profiles on places like LinkedIn, Facebook, and translator sites like Proz.com. They will usually list their credentials here, possibly in more detail than in places like their Babelcube profile. These sites will also have customer reviews, recommendations, and more details on their translation work history.

Translators can also complete quizzes on these translation sites to demonstrate their language proficiency. Check to see if they have done any and what their scores were. Also check the people who left them reviews or recommendations to verify if they actually worked for them or not. In a few cases, I've seen reviews of translators that were left by other translators, so checking out the reviewers is also a good idea.

A lack of history doesn't mean that a translator isn't qualified, but it doesn't provide you with any independent verification either.

It is important to do your due diligence. The last thing you want is poor reviews because of a bad translation. The name readers remember will be yours, not the translator's. A bad experience means they are unlikely to buy your books again.

Verifiable Experience and Results

Ideally you will choose an experienced translator who has already translated books that have sold well enough to have reviews. Look on book sites such as Amazon, Barnes & Noble, Kobo, Apple, and Google Play for books translated by the translator. Be sure to look on the foreign language site rather than the English one. For a German translator, look on the German Amazon store (Amazon.de) rather than the American store, as you will be more likely to find book reviews there.

Reviews can be tricky, so it takes a bit of assessment to evaluate them. A red flag for me is any mention of translation in the review. Any comments of poor translations are reason for further review because the translation should be invisible to a reader and never pull them out of the story. If it is a good translation, the reader will not even mention it is a translated work.

Regional Variations

As mentioned earlier, many languages have different dialects, and there are some you will prefer over others based on global popularity as well as the market you are targeting. Spanish is a good example.

It is so important that I want to reinforce it here. Spanish spoken in Spain differs from the Spanish spoken in Mexico. Mexican Spanish also differs from South American Spanish. Some people might tell you that you have a bad translation, but it could be simply due to variations in the dialect. It might be unfair, but it is the reality, and you don't want your book to suffer bad reviews or poor sales because of it.

Look for different dialects and decide which/where to focus. Spanish spoken and written in Spain is much different than the Spanish in Latin America, for instance. There are even differences between Latin American Spanish and Mexican Spanish. It is critical that you choose the appropriate translator for the right market.

European Spanish will be more widely accepted in Latin American than the other way around. It's not that the differences are not understood, but when something is written differently than your dialect, it can really pull you out of the story. And occasionally there will be words known in one region but not in another. There are many British words not used by Americans, for example.

If you are a worldwide bestseller, then you can produce multiple translations to address these differences in dialect. Otherwise, you have to compromise somewhat and make a conscious choice to target one language dialect over another.

In Spanish, for instance, I prefer to use a European Spanish translation over a Mexican one. A good Spanish translator will still try to minimize the differences to produce a translation in "neutral" Spanish, but there will always be word options that require a choice one way or another. The translation won't be ideal for all markets, but it will please most while still being acceptable to the majority of readers in other dialects.

It's just not practical to have a version for every dialect, so choose the dominant one. This is not always based on the same criteria, so ask a few native speakers for guidance. Often, it's the mother country, but not always.

For Portuguese, it's a little different. I have chosen to translate into Brazilian Portuguese because it represents such a huge market in comparison to European Portuguese. I am aware that this choice will likely alienate some European Portuguese readers, but I have chosen to focus on what I believe is the more profitable market of the two.

I also choose to use European French, knowing that my choice may not appeal to French Canadian readers (in itself a sizeable market). I also know that each market has socioeconomic considerations that must be weighed, and my decisions have trade-offs.

Other authors may decide differently based on their target markets and assumptions about the future, so while my assumptions hold true for my books, they might not be the right approach for you.

Evaluating Reviews on Translated Books

Even good reviews of translations can be problematic. Just as with any book, sometimes the reviews have been left by friends or family of the translator, who are just trying to help the book get off to a good start. Usually they will mention things like a great translation. Most readers never think about a translation, so any reviews mentioning how fantastic the translation is should also be ignored.

Online Presence

You will also want to search for information on the translator to see what sort of online presence they have. A professional presence such as a website is a good sign, and can also provide more information on their areas of specialty and rates.

It is also a good idea to check the various national translator associations such as the American Translators Association (ATA) to see if your translator is a member. Membership is not a measure of quality, but it does indicate certain minimum standards. Some of the websites like Proz.com also have translator ratings based on language proficiency from various language tests they offer. Following these steps should considerably narrow your search.

Evaluating a Translation Sample

Most translation platforms operate in a similar fashion. The translator provides a very short sample to the author. If the author accepts it, the translator then produces a longer sample, usually about 10 pages. This does not have to be the first 10 pages of the book, and some authors will provide a 10-page sample from the middle of their book that has particular terms or phrases that could be either difficult or produce many variations.

Once you get a sample, find a reader who is a native speaker in the destination language. Ideally this will be a reader or writer in your genre who can evaluate whether the translation reads and flows well and confirm that it is well-written on its own and true to your original tone and style.

This gets kind of tricky, because how can you tell if the evaluator is qualified to judge whether a translation is quality work or not? If the evaluator is also a literary translator with good reviews and lots of experience, then you can usually take them at their word.

But since you are just starting out, you likely don't know other literary translators. One useful place to find evaluators is large author forums, or wherever authors hang out. It's possible there are multilingual authors who will have the knowledge in the same language pair. They can evaluate grammar, word choice, the general quality of the translation sample, and whether or not it is true to the original version.

You can also find a second translator to evaluate the sample on sites like Proz or Upwork. Just be sure that your evaluator is at least at the same experience level as your potential translator. This is a bit of a catch-22 if you don't know the language. This is why it's so important to verify translator credentials as objective evidence of their competence.

If you are asking a friend to evaluate your sample, proceed with caution if the destination language isn't their native tongue, or if they haven't lived in that country for a long time. Unless they regularly read in the destination language and genre, their assessment may mislead you.

If possible, try to get several opinions on the translation quality. Be specific in what you are asking them to look at. You want to ensure that the translation is not just a strict translation, but rather one that captures the tone and emotion of the original text. Your book is a form of entertainment, so while the book must convey the meaning, it must also replicate the passion of your romance novel or the pulse-pounding terror of your horror novel.

You can overlook minor typographical errors to some extent if you have chosen a translator team since the final book will be proofread by the second translator. On the other hand, a translator who provides you with a sample of their work without having carefully reviewed their work should be cause for concern. You want a translator who puts the same level of care and attention into their work as you do, because your reputation will depend on it.

All of these screening steps take time but they are well worth it. If you end up with a bad translation because you didn't screen, the implications can be significant and permanent.

If you paid a flat fee for the translation, then you are out the money. But if you chose a royalty share deal and you accept the translation, then you are obligated to publish it under your name and your author brand. You are also locked into a multi-year contract with the original translator for the length of the contract term and cannot unpublish and/or redo the translation with another translator until the contract term is up.

Translator Screening Checklist

I use the following checklist to screen for translators. There are always exceptions to the rules, but this checklist narrows down the potential pool to candidates who meet certain minimum standards:

- Professional accreditations, such as membership in professional translator associations such as the American Translators Association or equivalent in the translator's country. Depending on the country, this may or may not indicate the translator has passed proficiency tests. However, membership does indicate to me that they are serious about their work and career as a translator.
- Formal education, such as a bachelor or master's degree in translation. Be sure to check the name of the equivalent degree in different countries. Sometimes they are under different names, such as a philosophy degree in France, for example.
- Translator's native tongue is the destination language, and translator is college-level fluent in the source language (at a minimum, the same reading level as your books are written in).
- Translator's profile in the source language is well-written in the source language, with no spelling and grammatical mistakes in the profile or your subsequent communications.
- Verifiable professional credentials, such as membership in translation associations, reviews, or participation on Proz.com, for example.
- Prior experience in literary translations and good online book reviews of the translated work.
- Reviews by other authors. Hint: read carefully between the lines.
- Mention of translation quality in a reader review. I immediately reject these because a good translation

should not be noticed. The review comment indicates either a bad translation, or in the case of good translation, a fake review.
- Translator has too many projects on the go (could impact quality or timing).
- Translator's interest in your work. I have noticed that translators that only do certain genres or want to read your book first before making a decision are the best translators. They take only projects that interest them and that they think will do well. To me, this shows professionalism.
- Where they live. If they have been away from their home country for many years (where the language is spoken), they might not be up to date on the latest phrases, slang, and idioms. This might be more important in contemporary romance than historical fiction, so weigh accordingly.
- Sample translations are important but with some caveats. You can find a reader to check if there are grammatical or translation errors. Having a friend who speaks the language is helpful, but if they don't always read in that language or genre, you won't necessarily know if it is well-written or not. It should be used in evaluating the translation but never as the sole criteria.
- Trust your instincts. Sometimes people look great on paper, but your gut tells you otherwise. Go with that feeling.

8

PUBLISHING YOUR TRANSLATED BOOK

Checking & Publishing

Title

Choose your title in consultation with your translator. You don't want a literal translation, but one that not only captures the essence of the book and entices readers to buy it, but also the genre. Genres and categories often differ in other languages, so check out the larger sales platforms in the destination language and look at how they group books. Also, in many languages, the subtitle is the genre. French thrillers are often subtitled "policier/thriller", Dutch ones "thriller", and so on.

One important consideration is whether or not to include metadata in both the title and the subtitle. It is worthwhile explaining to the translator the advantages of including key search terms, but I recommend that you come up with specific examples and preferably samples to share with the translator so that they get the idea. Rather than offering one title and subtitle, provide them with some choices that contain your desired metadata and have them tell you why they are or aren't suitable. Having the right keywords in your title and subtitle makes a huge difference in your book's discoverability, so you want to take full advantage of it where possible.

Note that I am not saying you should have a 60-word title incorporating every search term you can think of. That just cheapens the look of your book. But if your book is a romance, include that word and the subgenre in the subtitle at least, and use the same style as the other books in the genre.

This should be the appropriate terms used in that language since categories vary by language. For a French translation of your contemporary romance novel, for instance, look at French stores such as fnac.com and Amazon.fr and see how the books are categorized. Incorporate the most suitable category name as part of the subtitle, and you have just added one more way for French romance readers to find your book.

I also recommend discussing your title discoverability goals with your translator at the outset. This gives them time to think about the title while they are translating the book. A good translator will come up with a title that not only shows up on search results, but entices the reader and conveys the reading experience they will get.

Manuscript

Regardless of your translation arrangements, you will follow the same steps to get your book formatted and ready for publishing. Make sure that the formatted text retains any language-specific characters such as accents. Punctuation and spacing can differ in other languages too. Be especially careful when copying or reviewing your manuscript to ensure that you don't inadvertently change anything.

Don't forget to add your translator as contributor under your author name, as well as listing her as a contributor on the publishing platforms when you publish your book.

Cover

You will need a new cover. Traditional publishers often design different covers for each major market to suit local preferences. A U.S. cover for a romance novel might be more explicit than the cover for the same novel in the U.K., for example. Publishers adapt covers to appeal to local tastes.

As an independent author, you only have the option to upload one cover per book, unless you create two different editions. This probably isn't necessary for just marketing reasons.

However, sometimes covers are changed to address more conservative values or even laws in other countries. Unless you have a racy cover on your erotica book or have overtly political images on a war story, you likely don't have to worry about making changes.

In most cases, you can keep the same image and just change the type on your cover to that of the foreign language. Your cover designer will likely do it for free or a very small fee.

If you are doing paperbacks, you will also need to change the spine width to adjust for a larger or smaller number of pages in the translated version.

Publishing

Aside from checking that language-specific characters are retained in your formatted book, you will want to also check that the title and metadata have reproduced properly with language-specific accents, for example, in the description fields and titles on each sales platform.

Even when the data entry fields appear correct, they might lose formatting when actually published on the retailer site, so check them again after the book is published.

I find that CreateSpace sometimes does not replicate the accents in French and other titles. It seems that sometimes it works and sometimes it doesn't. It's very important to have the title appear correctly so that it shows up properly in search results when people look for it. If you find weird language-formatting errors in your title and are unable to correct them after a few tries, contact CreateSpace and ask them to correct it.

Other than that, there are no differences in formatting and file generation for your translated book.

Launch Strategy

It is a good idea to discuss your launch strategy and timing with your translator to see if they can help, or at least provide feedback on your plans. Another area to ask for assistance is translation of advertising copy if you are planning to do any advertising, like Facebook ads for instance. If you or your translators know of any book bloggers, I recommend reaching out to them by offering a giveaway to join your mailing list. This way you can start a mailing list in that specific language. This is covered in detail in the next chapter.

I keep separate mailing lists for each language. Segmented mailing lists allow you to send language-specific new release notifications and updates only for the language edition that pertains to them. It also makes it easier to monitor opens, clicks, and other performance measures by each language.

9

MARKETING & ADVERTISING

Your newly published book has visibility in the first few days and weeks after release, but then what? Before long it fades into obscurity and is lost amongst the sea of books. Your books are supplanted by every new release until they are buried and no one knows to look for them.

While there are fewer books out in non-English markets, there are also fewer readers. You have a great cover and a catchy blurb, but all that is no good if nobody can find your book. What can you do to make your book stand out?

The good news is that many of the things you do with your English language books can be done in other markets. And, since these markets are less mature than the English language market, there is less competition, not only for advertising sites but also bidding for ads. Your cost per click will likely be lower on Facebook and similar sites.

However, because there are fewer readers, it could be harder to reach them. The lower number of readers are due both to permanent and temporary differences from the English language market. First, the number of readers in most other languages (essentially a permanent difference), and later adoption of eBooks or shopping online (temporary difference). Non-English markets are ripe for disruption though, so it's only a matter of time before things get more competitive. That's why it's vital to get visible in these markets while it's still easy to do so.

But how to gain visibility when you don't speak the language?

Translators as Marketers

The logical choice would be to ask someone who speaks the language. The first person that comes to mind is the translator, since she is already very familiar and involved with your book. In fact, Babelcube suggests that your translator should be heavily involved in promotion. On the face of it this makes sense.

On the other hand, your translator probably isn't as knowledgeable about advertising and marketing as you are, especially when it comes to promoting a book. And, as we know, most people don't like to do promotion in the first place. Unless you define what you mean by "marketing", even an enthusiastic translator will be reluctant to take this on.

Many translators also feel they have already done a lot of work by simply translating the work, and I agree with them. You might find excellent translators who do not want to do any marketing. Sometimes it could mean that they are uncomfortable with writing marketing copy or fear that you will ask them to aggressively market the translated book. They don't want to blog all day about your book.

In fact, this isn't what I expected from them anyway. What I want is to prepare the marketing copy myself, in my language. I only need help for the "last mile" to get my copy translated into the destination language. Finding blogs and promotion sites would also be helpful, but I can do that myself, and contacts at most of these sites will know enough English to answer my inquiries. It's all about what you ask for and being as specific as possible.

Now I know that if I provide the marketing copy to translate or ask specific questions that they can answer, most translators are happy to help. And if they aren't, that's okay too. First and foremost, you want the best translation possible for your book. I'd rather have that than a talented marketer promoting a mediocre translation. But if you can find both a talented translator and a natural marketer in the same person, it's a bonus.

Marketing is a scary thing for most people. But when you break it down into its components, it's not as daunting as it first seems. Knowing the specifics goes a long way to alleviating someone's fear of the unknown, so I think it's better for the author to do the parts they are knowledgeable in, and leverage the translator's talents for things like local knowledge and language requirements.

I try to do as much of the work as possible, so that all they have to do is translate the advertising copy, blurbs, and so on, and maybe redirect me if I am headed in the wrong direction. I feel confident in preparing advertising copy in my native language and determining where and how to market. I bounce ideas off the translator for validation and often get back very useful suggestions.

Often I just provide the English ad to my translator with a request to translate the dozen or so words in the ad. This way I can also get their reaction on whether the ad graphics "translate well" for their market—whether the image and call to action is catchy enough. Then I incorporate the translated copy and voila, I have a translated ad that is ready to use in Facebook ads or other promotions.

I share my promotional goals with my translator and also prepare an information sheet with the book's title, blurb, graphics, and buy links. That makes it almost effortless for the translator to share and promote the translated book. In general, I try to ask the translators for help only in areas where I lack knowledge and confidence. There is no one-fits-all solution, so adjust as needed.

Ideally, it is a joint effort, with the author providing advertising copy to be translated, and the author and translator working together to find promotional sites. I believe promotional sites are only a temporary way to discover books until the big sales platforms such as Amazon, Apple, Google Play, and Kobo offer more pay per click advertising or promotional opportunities on their sites, just as they are starting to do in the English market. This makes it easy because all you need is some translated copy, a translated cover, appropriate keyword targeting, and you're all set.

Book Promotion Sites

Until then, you will need to find other ways to gain visibility, such as book blogs and book advertising sites. Ideally, your translator will know some of these sites, but if not, you might have to provide some guidance on how to find them.

You can also find them yourself. Search terms in that language for things like eBook bargains or similar phrases should identify some key sites. This is where Google Translate comes in handy since you can translate almost any website into your language to see whether it is a fit for your promotional needs.

Facebook ads could also be effective and the market is not as saturated as it is for English language books. With lower competition, the cost might be more reasonable. However, the effectiveness depends upon the popularity of the platform itself in that particular language.

For example, I ran a Facebook ad on a new Dutch release and despite the popularity of my books there, it had a very low engagement. I know that the book is popular and the cover resonates with readers. I targeted the demographic that reads my books. I also believe Facebook is popular there too. Yet it wasn't effective. The problem could be my advertising copy or call to action, or maybe I didn't target the right demographic. It's always hard to know with advertising, but it's a little more challenging to evaluate your results when you are advertising in a foreign language.

Marketing and advertising costs can really add up if you aren't careful. If you are designing ads to use on sites like Facebook, the best way to approach it is to try a few variations of your advertisement and do some split testing to see which one works better. Split-testing is when you run two almost identical ads at the same time, usually with only one or a few differences so you can narrow down what works and what doesn't. Bid low to start, and once you've found an ad that gets the best number of clicks, stop all the other ads and spend your money on the successful one. This will save you money in the long run.

No matter how you advertise, it can quickly erode your profits or even put you in a loss position unless you stick to your budget, carefully review and assess your results, and modify where needed.

And, as you can imagine, it is easier to profit when you have more than one book out because if readers like your book, you will get sell-through. For this reason, I recommend waiting until you have a few books out in a particular language before you start advertising.

The best billboard is still the back of your book, just like it is in English. Capturing a reader's attention is easiest while you still have them in your ecosystem. Use a call to action at the end of your book to either buy the next one or to sign up for your new release notifications.

The back of the book is like Manhattan real estate—a prime location to communicate with your reader. This takes on even greater importance when you don't speak the language since your ability to blog or otherwise communicate in a language you don't speak is limited. All you have to do is provide something that requires no translation: a link to the next book. I always ensure that my links are configured to show all my books with the translation language first, so that the reader doesn't see a bunch of English books first instead.

This is a more passive form of advertising but probably the most effective one. Anyone who has read to the end of your book has almost certainly enjoyed it, so these are potentially your most loyal readers, the ones who will buy your next book the minute it is released. They will also be the most likely to recommend your books to their friends.

One Website or Many?

As with everything, there are always trade-offs between perfection and practicality.

I have one website for all languages of my book, with separate tabs for each language. Other authors use a page per book, with each foreign edition of that title listed on the same page. While this seems like a neat and tidy way to organize your books, it probably isn't how a reader is going to look for your books. More importantly, once a reader finds me, I want them to see and buy all the books I have in their language. For that reason, I recommend one section of your website for each language, with all titles listed there.

Some authors have a separate website for each language. An obvious disadvantage is multiple website domain names and added expense. It also makes for more work. Another downside to this is that your website traffic will be spread among many sites, which means you won't rank as high in search results. I am not sure how many people will find your website and then follow on to your books through an organic search, but more traffic is always good.

Social media

You probably already have a Facebook author page where you provide updates and talk about new releases. Some authors have created separate Facebook pages for each language. This is ideal— that is, as long as you have an assistant in each language to manage the page. Some bestselling authors do this, and the advantage is a cohesive, organized page that talks directly to readers in that language. As with most things, it is a trade-off. If you're making a million dollars a year, it might be worthwhile to take these extra steps and engage even more with your fans.

Don't forget that a Facebook page, unlike your website, isn't something you control. Things can change overnight, and often they do. I don't recommend spending a lot of money curating something that could disappear tomorrow. Better to engage those readers by getting them to sign up to your email list, where you can control the content and the delivery system.

Most of my translators are happy to translate blog posts and newsletters for the books they have translated because it benefits them in the long run when the book performs well. Just make sure you don't overdo it and ask for too much. A new release newsletter is one thing, but if you plan on regular monthly communication with your subscribers in that language, you should expect to pay the translator for this ongoing translation work.

10

CONCLUSION

I've included some handy checklists in the appendix so that you can easily refer back to them as needed. Most of the pointers are common sense, but it's easy to lose track because there are so many things to think of.

Your intellectual rights and how you monetize them are important as well as who you work with. Markets can and will change, but market fundamentals and how to assess them won't. Knowing what to look for is key, and I believe I've given you the tools to do that.

This book was written with the intent of providing a concise overview of translation opportunities today along with practical advice on how to make informed choices. It is an evolving marketplace but one that I think holds vast opportunities for entrepreneurial authors.

I hope I've convinced you to take the first few steps towards getting your books into new languages and markets, or at least given you something to think about.

If you enjoyed the book please consider leaving a short review. I love getting feedback because it helps me to continuously improve and also tailor my books to my readers' needs. More than anything though, I want to share my experiences with as many authors as possible. It's a small world with big opportunities that are ours if we want them.

Dream Big and Happy Translating!

11

APPENDIX - CHECKLISTS

These checklists are provided here for easy reference. It's best to start with the first checklist (choosing language markets) and proceed through each checklist in order.

Choosing Languages and Markets

Ideal markets have two or more of the following features:

HP or High prices – books command high selling prices

HG or High growth – reading is widespread and steady or growing in popularity

LC or Low competition – a low number of books to meet demand

LM or Large Market – a large potential market of readers

Genre – Chosen genre and sub-genre are among the most popular ones in that particular language and market

Choosing Fee Structures – Flat Fee vs. Royalty

Flat Fee

Pros

- You own the translation outright. You are free to distribute to all sales channels or just one without consulting with the translator or impacting their earnings.
- You continue to hold exclusive derivative rights for other formats such as audiobooks, paperbacks, or other things like movie options, so you can immediately exploit these rights and earn more money faster.
- Pricing flexibility. You can choose to make the first book free or cheap for marketing purposes, something that would be unfair to your translator under a royalty share basis.
- Eliminates the need for the tedious record-keeping required under a royalty share agreement.
- Minimizes risk of legal disputes since the contract ends once the book is delivered.
- Can be the cheapest option for you if your book sells well.
- You will get your translation completed quickly since the translator will prioritize it as "paid" work rather than a royalty share with its longer payment timeframe and uncertainty.

Cons

- You bear the cost of the translation, which can be prohibitively expensive and add up if you have many books.

- You might never recoup your investment. Book prices can drop, subscription models changed, and competition can increase, preventing you from recovering your costs.
- Less incentive for an unethical translator to provide a quality product as there is no revenue at risk once the final product is delivered. You might not realize there are edit or quality issues until you get bad reviews.
- Translator might not be motivated to help you with marketing and promotion in the foreign market once they have been paid in full.

Royalty Share (on a third-party translation platform)

Pros

- The translation platform deals with the record-keeping, payments, and taxes.
- The translation platform can intercede on your behalf if there are contract issues such as late delivery or non-performance.
- Work for hire contracts protect your intellectual property rights.
- Once the term is up, you get all subsequent royalties and can exploit your intellectual rights.
- Very cost effective and low risk.

Cons

- The translation platform takes a percentage of net revenue, leaving less money to split between you and the translator.

- You cannot exploit your subsidiary rights, such as audiobooks that are based on the translation until the contract term is over.
- There is a middleman between you and the published books, limiting your ability to set prices, categories, and use platform-specific advertising programs to directly promote your books on some sales platforms.

Translator Screening Checklist

- Professional accreditations, such as membership in professional translator associations, for example, American Translators Association. Depending on the country, this may or may not indicate the translator has passed proficiency tests. However, membership does indicate to me that they are serious about their work and career as a translator.
- Formal education, such as a bachelor or master's degree in translation. Be sure to check the name of the equivalent degree in different countries. Sometimes they are under different names, such as a philosophy degree in France.
- Translator's native tongue is the destination language, and translator is college-level fluent in the source language (at a minimum, the same reading level as your books are written in).
- Translator's profile in the source language is well-written in the source language, with no spelling and grammatical mistakes in the profile or your subsequent communications.
- Verifiable professional credentials, such as membership in translation associations, reviews, or participation on Proz.com.
- Prior experience in literary translations and good online book reviews of the translated work

- Reviews by other authors. Hint: read between the lines.
- Mention of translation quality in a reader review. I immediately reject these because a good translation should not be noticed. The review comment indicates either a bad translation, or in the case of good translation, a fake review.
- Translator has too many projects on the go (could impact quality or timing).
- Translator's interest in your work. Translators that only do certain genres or want to read your book first before making a decision are the best translators. They take only projects that interest them and that they think will do well. To me, this shows professionalism.
- Where they live. If they have been away from their home country for many years (where the language is spoken), they might not be up to date on the latest phrases, slang, and idioms. This might be more important in contemporary romance than historical fiction, so weigh accordingly.
- Sample translations are important but with some caveats. You can ask a reader to check if there are grammatical or translation errors. Having a friend who speaks the language is helpful, but if they don't always read in that language or genre, you won't necessarily know if it is well-written or not. It should be used in evaluating the translation but never as the sole criteria.
- Trusting your instincts. Sometimes people look great on paper, but your gut tells you otherwise. Go with that feeling.

www.ingramcontent.com/pod-product-compliance
Lightning Source LLC
Chambersburg PA
CBHW060536080526
44586CB00012B/759